James

New Testament Guides

Series Editor

Andrew T. Lincoln

Other New Testament Guides available from T&T Clark:

James

John S. Kloppenborg

t&tclark

LONDON • NEW YORK • OXFORD • NEW DELHI • SYDNEY

T&T CLARK
Bloomsbury Publishing Plc
50 Bedford Square, London, WC1B 3DP, UK
1385 Broadway, New York, NY 10018, USA
29 Earlsfort Terrace, Dublin 2, Ireland

BLOOMSBURY, T&T CLARK and the T&T Clark logo are
trademarks of Bloomsbury Publishing Plc

First published in Great Britain 2022

Cover design: Charlotte James

A catalogue record for this book is available from the British Library.

Library of Congress Cataloging-in-Publication Data
Names: Kloppenborg, John S., 1951- author.
Title: James / John S. Kloppenborg.
Description: London ; New York : T&T Clark, [2022] |
Series: New Testament guides | Includes bibliographical
references and index. | Summary: "This volume offers a concise and
accessible introduction to a New Testament text, in this case aimed specifically
at undergraduate-level students"– Provided by publisher.
Identifiers: LCCN 2021016638 (print) | LCCN 2021016639 (ebook) |
ISBN 9780567471185 (pb) | ISBN 9780567481405 (hb) | ISBN 9780567302106
(epdf) | ISBN 9780567703965 (epub)
Subjects: LCSH: Bible. James.–Criticism, interpretation, etc.
Classification: LCC BS2785.52 .K56 2022 (print) |
LCC BS2785.52 (ebook) | DDC 227/.9106–dc23
LC record available at https://lccn.loc.gov/2021016638
LC ebook record available at https://lccn.loc.gov/2021016639

ISBN: HB: 978-0-5674-8140-5
         PB: 978-0-5674-7118-5
         ePDF: 978-0-5673-0210-6
         ePUB: 978-0-5677-0396-5

Typeset by Integra Software Services Pvt. Ltd.
Printed and bound in Great Britain

To find out more about our authors and books visit www.bloomsbury.com
and sign up for our newsletters.

CONTENTS

PREFACE

This volume is meant as an introduction to the letter of James, not a summary of all that it has to say. As will quickly become clear, this short letter of 109 verses presents the interpreter with a host of issues and puzzles, features that are at once congenial and irritating. The path that this letter took on its way to incorporation into the canon of the New Testament was unusually complicated and in fact rather puzzling. It seems to have been largely unknown until the beginning of the third century CE, and this in turn raised serious suspicions about its authorship, suspicions that persisted until at least the fourth century, and which then resurfaced in the sixteenth. The manuscript history is also peculiar when set beside the manuscript histories of the canonical gospels and Pauline letters; it not only appears later among papyri with New Testament contents but lacks entirely the so-called Western witnesses.

For much of its recent history James stood in the shadow of Paul and the Pauline letters. Most know of Luther's famous pronouncement on James, that it was 'an epistle of straw', but fewer know the critiques of James by Erasmus and Cajetan, and several other much more challenging assessments by Luther. As it turns out the critiques of James that were leveled in the sixteenth century were prescient in the sense that they have set much of the research agenda in the twentieth and twenty-first centuries. The authorship, date, and provenance of James are still very much under debate, as they had been from the third century onwards. It is not entirely resolved what kind of text James is: a loose collection of wisdom sayings? a real letter? a diatribe? And irrespective of whether it is a genuine letter by James of Jerusalem or a pseudepigrapher writing in James's name, does it envisage as its readers Jews, Jewish Christians, or Gentile Christians? Or perhaps it does not really envisage any particular readership at all. As a Christian text—if that is what James is—it is peculiar that James makes no allusions to what might be thought to be the core beliefs and practices of the early Christ movement.

These are just some of the introductory issues that the interpreter must confront in approaching James.

Throughout I will use the name 'James' to refer both to the author of the letter and to the letter itself. This should not be taken to imply that I believe that the author is James of Jerusalem, the brother of Jesus. In fact, I do not. But to refer to the author and the work as that of 'James' is less clumsy than repetitively referring to 'the author' and 'the author's work'. This book will include quite a bit of Greek, always transliterated into Roman characters. James presents some of the best Greek of NT books, *and* it is replete with neologisms, words that are rare or unattested in Greek before the first century CE, along with some very archaic vocabulary. Understanding James means coming to terms with his odd lexical profile. English translations of James simply do not convey the oddness of his language.

All translations of James are my own. The translations of other biblical texts are from the NRSV. Readers will note that I have not opted to use gender-inclusive language in rendering James's Greek into English. This is because James himself does not. He often uses *anēr* ('man', 'male') where we might expect *anthrōpos* ('person') and to the extent that we can reconstruct his intended readership, it is male. For that reason, I have also rendered *adelphoi mou agapētoi* as 'my beloved brothers' rather than 'my beloved brothers and sisters', with the NRSV and other modern translations that are designed for liturgical use. Of course, once James was incorporated into the canon, and placed alongside 1 Peter or, more distantly, 1 Corinthians, both of which imagined ecclesial communities that included women and men (and slaves and children), it became possible to read James's rather androcentric language more generously, as including women. But this volume is in the first instance interested in the original author and his imagination of his addressees.

I am grateful for Andrew Lincoln for first inviting me to contribute this volume, and to Christina Gousopoulos for proofreading the manuscript and saving me from a variety of errors.

ABBREVIATIONS

The abbreviations for Periodicals and Series are those of Billie Jean Collins, Bob Buller, and John F. Kutsko, *The SBL Handbook of Style: For Biblical Studies and Related Disciplines*. Second ed. Atlanta, GA: SBL Press, 2014.

In addition, the following abbreviations are used.

CIIP I/1 Cotton, Hannah M., Leah Di Segni, Werner Eck, Benjamin Isaac, Alla Kushnir-Stein, Haggai Misgav, Jonathan J. Price, Israel Roll, and Ada Yardeni, eds. *Jerusalem, Part 1:1–704*. Vol. 1/1 of *Corpus Inscriptionum Iudaeae/Palaestinae: A Multi-Lingual Corpus of the Inscriptions from Alexander to Muhammad*. Berlin and New York: Walter de Gruyter, 2010.

GRA III Kloppenborg, John S. *Ptolemaic and Early Roman Egypt*. Vol. III of *Greco-Roman Associations: Texts, Translations, and Commentary*. BZNW 246. Berlin and New York: Walter de Gruyter, 2020. doi:10.1515/9783110710397.

LW Pelikan, Jaroslav, and Helmut T. Lehmann, gen. eds. *Luther's Works*. Edited by H.C. Oswald, H.J. Grimm, H.T. Lehmann, and Joel W. Lundeen. Saint Louis: Concordia; Philadelphia: Fortress, 1955–86.

MAMA Calder, William M., E. Herzfeld, S. Guyer, and C.W.M. Cox, eds. *Monumenta Asiae Minoris antiqua*. London: Manchester University Press, 1928–.

SVF von Arnim, Hans Friedrich August. *Stoicorum veterum fragmenta*. Leipzig and Stuttgart: Teubner, 1903–1924.

WA   Luther, Martin. *D. Martin Luthers Werke: Kritische Gesamtausgabe (Weimarer Ausgabe)*, ed. J. K. F. Knaake et al. 73 vols. Weimar: H. Böhlaus, 1883–.

1

Approaching James

When one interprets any piece of early Christian literature, context matters. It matters in what company a text is placed, for that company will affect how the text is read. Does one read the canonical gospels only in relation to each other? Or only alongside other Christian texts? Or in the context of the biographies produced by Greek and Latin writers? Or in the context supplied by accounts of Hebrew prophets? Or in the context of the canon of the Christian Bible? It's not that there is only one appropriate context. But some are more helpful than others, and as we will see, some contexts work to narrow or perhaps even distort interpretive possibilities. James, a relatively short letter of 108 verses (1749 words), has been read in a variety of contexts, and some of those contexts work to disguise James's contributions to the history and thought of the early Christ movement and to narrow its interpretation significantly.

Modern editions of the New Testament place James at the head of the 'Catholic' or 'General Epistles'—James, 1–2 Peter, 1–2–3 John, and Jude—that is, letters purported to come from Jesus's closest associates. I say 'purported', because modern analysis has made it clear that the two Petrine letters were not written by Jesus's disciple Peter. The two letters were not even written by the same author. It is impossible to connect 1–2–3 John with John the son of Zebedee. The authorship of the letter of Jude is also very much in question; what is clearer is that 2 Peter, which belongs to the second century CE, made use of the letter of Jude.

The Catholic letters are now found sandwiched between Paul's genuine letters, the Pastorals (1–2 Timothy, Titus) and Hebrews on one side, and the Apocalypse of John on the other. Because at 37,400 words, the Pauline corpus and Hebrews are almost five times as long as the Catholic letters (7583 words), the current arrangement of NT books gives extraordinary weight to Paul and much less prominence to the Catholic letters. It is hardly surprising that the volume of commentary on the Pauline letters outweighs that on the Catholic letters and James by several magnitudes.

The arrangement of books in the modern NT canon is not, however, the arrangement found in most Greek manuscripts of the New Testament, which regularly placed Acts and the Catholic letters together. Both Codex Vaticanus in the fourth century and Codex Alexandrinus in the fifth, along with almost all later Greek manuscripts, place the Acts and the Catholic letters *before* Paul's letters. The same arrangement is found in the lists of canonical texts in such Greek writers as Athanasius and Cyril of Jerusalem. Codex Sinaiticus in the fourth century differs in this regard, by placing Acts and the Catholic letters together, but immediately *after* Paul's letters and Hebrews and before the Apocalypse, the letter of Barnabas, and the Shepherd of Hermas. In both of these sequences, Acts and the Catholic letters are treated as a single unit, which creates another interpretive context. The association of the Catholic letters with Acts has the effect of underwriting the authority of the Catholic letters by featuring letters from four disciples who appear prominently in the first fifteen chapters of Acts. Some have even suggested that placing the Catholic letters before Paul's letters was to protect against extreme interpretations of Paulinism.

The canonical location of James provides one context for thinking about James. But of course, this has to do with decisions made by fourth- and fifth-century writers and copyists and how they conceived of the structure of the New Testament as a whole. Those choices, however interesting and telling they might be, do not tell us much about how James was read on its own terms, before its incorporation into the group of Catholic letters and before their incorporation to the NT canon.

For most of the nineteenth and twentieth centuries, interpreters of James typically read the letter in another context, not in conjunction with Acts, but as a counterpoint to the letters of Paul. Until recently, the majority of monographs and articles on James focused on a single section, Jas 2:14–26 and its supposed confrontation with Pauline theology in Galatians and Romans. This fixation on Paul also led scholars to focus on James's 'theology', as if James were self-evidently a theological tractate comparable to, and in conversation with, Galatians and Romans. Yet as Karl-Wilhelm Niebuhr rightly observes, the structure of James's letter hardly suggests that his primary concern was either theology or the relation of faith to deeds. Instead, it is a work about ethics, even if one can deduce some of the theological views that inform James's ethical stances (Niebuhr 2009).

The opening section of James offers a partial table of contents. The list of topics mooted in chapter 1 includes the search of wisdom and how properly to approach God; the pointlessness of pursuing wealth and the dangers of pleasure and desire; and the importance of self-control and the willingness to hear and to perform the 'perfect law of freedom'. True piety, says James, is 'to watch over orphans and widows in their distress, and to guard oneself uncontaminated from the world' (Jas 1:27).

In the light of the introduction James provided for his letter, it is mistaken to focus only on Jas 2:14–26, as though this were the core of his message. On the contrary, the common focus for the letter might be better conceived as what James calls 'piety' (*thrēskeia*, 1:26–27, often mistranslated as 'religion'). Piety begins from a conception of God as the source of all that is good and as a generous benefactor. It also involves psychagogy, that is, the cultivation of the soul. It involves adopting the proper attitudes for approaching God, and awareness of the several impediments that cloud and obscure the perception of the Good, especially desire, pleasure, anger, and arrogance. When the appropriate conceptions of the self and God are in place, pious acts and a pious way of life follow: care for the poor; the rejection of favouritism; control of the tongue; suppression of envy; the rejection of injustice and arrogance, and the adoption of behaviour that nurtures the community.

Psychagogy thus entails both mental attitudes and moral actions. James is concerned with care of the poor and offers many critical comments on wealth and the wealthy (1:9–11). He objects to the sycophantic attitudes toward the rich and the actions that follow from such attitudes (2:1–13) and he decries the predatory practices of landlords toward their workers (5:1–6). James is not simply a list of do's and don'ts. On the contrary, he is worried about the way that the pursuit of luxury and good living infects and perverts the soul. These topics resonate with other early Christian texts, in particular Luke's gospel and especially the Shepherd of Hermas, both from the latter part of the first century CE or early second century.

The author of course has a paragraph on the relation of faith to deeds and declares that the faith that lacks the performance of corresponding deeds is unfruitful and indeed dead (2:20, 26). This is consistent with what is argued throughout the second chapter of James, that genuine faith issues in acts that are consistent with the Law, since piety for James entails both right beliefs and right actions. But James is also deeply concerned with speech ethics (3:1–12), the destructive nature and the causes of envy (3:13–4:10), and the arrogant and wilful behaviour of the wealthy (4:11–5:6). The letter ends with exhortations to patience (5:7–11), and a cluster of topics pertaining to conduct within the assembly (5:12–20).

Part of the reasons for the general neglect that James has suffered and for the narrowing of focus to Jas 2:14–26 alone can be traced to the sixteenth century. From almost the beginning, there had been persistent suspicions that James was a pseudepigraphon. It was in the sixteenth century, however, that these suspicions came to a head. Erasmus argued on stylistic grounds that the letter could not have been penned by the brother of Jesus, thought to be the first bishop of Jerusalem. Luther's Catholic opponent Cajetan concluded that the letter was not by an apostle. It was, however, Martin Luther who cast the gravest doubts on the worth of James, famously declaring it to be a 'letter of straw' ('Preface to the New Testament [1522]', LW 35:362). (Interestingly, Luther omitted this comment from the editions of his New Testament published after 1522). His deepest problem with James was theological: it lacked any mention of what Luther considered to be the heart of the gospel—reference to the death and resurrection of Jesus and mention of the spirit of Christ. James seemed to disagree with Paul and it hardly mentioned Jesus at all (only in 1:1 and 2:1). He even opined at one point that James might have been forged a letter in order to oppose Christians (LW 54:424). His most immoderate statement came in 1546 when he mused about throwing 'Jimmy' into the oven (LW 34:317).

Luther's comments on James had a lasting impact. For much of the twentieth century, James was either ignored, perhaps owing to Luther's verdict that it was an inferior product and maybe not even Christian, or it was deemed worthy of discussion only insofar as it seemed to disagree with Paul on the topic of faith and deeds. Or perhaps Jas 2:14–26 could be reconciled with Paul. It was not until 1998 that *Theologische Rundschau* featured a review article on James. This journal typically carries lengthy bibliographical articles on biblical books. It had featured extensive surveys of scholarship on Paul beginning in 1929, on John from 1955, and Acts from 1960. Only in 1998 did it finally published a review article on James (Hahn and Müller 1998).

Beginning in the last quarter of the twentieth century, the focus on James widened beyond Jas 2:14–16. Scholars began to pay addition to James as a whole. Important publications in the 1970s began to examine a variety of topics other than his views of faith and deeds: the social context presupposed by the letter; its theological background; the overall structure and rhetorical species of the letter; James's discourse on rich and poor; James as a document of second Temple Jewish wisdom; James as an example of epistolary paraenesis; James and the Jesus tradition, speech-ethics in James; James's critical view of the Roman institution of personal patronage; and James's urban perspective. Thus in 2004 Karl-Wilhelm Niebuhr could finally describe a 'New Perspective on James' (Niebuhr 2004):

> If one does not read the letter from a Pauline perspective, one would scarcely come to the conclusion that the argument about faith and works in 2:14–26 is its theological core and that it belongs to the context of early Christian debate about justification. Instead, the reader would seek the starting point for understanding the text at its beginning, the opening in which the author represents himself to his addressees as 'Jacob, slave of God and of the Lord Jesus Christ', and greets his addressees as 'the twelve tribes of the diaspora', and with an address comprised of admonitions addresses those who should persevere throughout their troubles.
>
> (Niebuhr 2004, 1040)

Ironically, Luther's criticisms of James have turned out to be almost a blueprint for the modern study of James: its authorship, its literary genre, the resources upon which it calls, and its addressees and function. It was Luther who mounted the most pungent attack on Jacobean authorship in the modern period. He was not the first to question the authenticity of James—Luther knew that there had been persistent doubts about the authenticity of James in antiquity. But he was the first to assemble a substantial set of objections to James. Many of those arguments would now be judged to be irrelevant or at least not probative. It will, however, be necessary to examine his, and other arguments against authenticity as well as defences of Jacobean authorship. This will be the task of Chapter 2.

Another second criticism of James by Luther had to do with its organization:

> He throws things together so chaotically that it seems to me that he must have been some good, pious man who took a few sayings from the disciples of the apostles and thus tossed them off on paper.
>
> (LW 35:397)

And again

> Besides, there's no order or method to the epistle. Now he discusses clothing and then he writes about wrath and is constantly shifting from one to the other.
>
> (LW 54:425)

As Chapter 3 will explain, Luther was measuring James against the theological tractates of Paul. He both exaggerated the coherence of Paul's letters and significantly underestimated the organization of James. What is more important, Luther entirely misjudged the genre of James; it is not a letter comparable to Paul's letters; instead, it is an example of epistolary paraenesis. Paraenetic literature often lacks an overarching structure, and sometimes does not even display organization of smaller clusters of sayings. When James is placed in the literary context to which it belongs, it becomes clear that it is in fact one of the *better* organized examples of epistolary paraenesis. James is very far from being 'chaotic'.

Luther's chief reasons for rejecting James were that it contradicted Paul on the issue of faith and works, that it failed to mention the death and resurrection of Jesus or the spirit of Christ, which Luther took to be the sine qua non of any writing that qualified as apostolic, and that it barely mentioned Christ.

> We should throw the Epistle of James out of this school, for it doesn't amount to much. It contains not a syllable about Christ. Not once does it mention Christ, except at the beginning.
>
> (LW 54:424)

The lack of mention of distinctively Christian beliefs and practices will occupy us in the final chapter. Luther's complaint that James 'contains not a syllable about Christ', however, needs reconsideration. As we will see in Chapter 4, James very clearly knows the Jewish Bible, although he quotes it verbatim only at 2:8, 11, 23 and 4:6. Elsewhere his use of the Bible is paraphrastic. This is in fact what one should expect of a work of Hellenistic Judaism, where authors preferred paraphrasis to verbatim quotation. As most commentators have noted, James is also far from ignorant of the Jesus tradition; his prose is suffused with allusions—always paraphrased—to the sayings of Jesus, and as has been recognized recently, mostly from the Q source. Thus, while James may say little *about* Christ, the Jesus tradition is present throughout James.

For the most part Luther seems to have grudgingly accepted James even though he judged it not to be the work of an apostle. But in *Table Talk* he even proposed a *non-Christian origin* of the book:

> I maintain that some Jew wrote it who probably heard about Christian people but never encountered any. Since he heard that Christians place great weight on faith in Christ, he thought, 'Wait a minute. I'll oppose them and urge works alone.' This he did. He wrote not a word about the suffering and resurrection of Christ, although this is what all the apostles preached about.
>
> (LW 54:424)

As Luther's comment shows, he placed great weight on Jas 2:14–26 and Paul's view of faith and deeds as theologically normative. And as we have seen, he was also struck by how little of explicit Christian teachings appeared. This continues to be an issue for interpreters. Is James, as some have suggested, a document originally penned by a Jewish writer and superficially Christianized? Was Luther right? The letter is addressed to the 'Twelve Tribes' in the diaspora. Is this a code word for Jewish Christians? Or all Christians? But if so, why is there no mention of characteristically Christian beliefs (about Jesus, for example), and practices, such as baptism and Eucharist? I will suggest in Chapter 5 another alternative: that the author, although he does not disguise his affiliation with the Jesus movement, addresses diaspora Jews in general—just as the prescript indicates. Thus, James envisages two sets of readers: Jews who belonged to the Jesus movement, who would have no difficulty in recognizing the many allusions to sayings of Jesus; and other Jews, for whom the letter offered a version of Jewish piety that was in conversation with popular philosophy, and a defense of the image of James of Jerusalem who was known to be a pious Jew who upheld the Torah.

Reading James as James

It has been said of the Gospel of John that everything we would like to know is uncertain and everything about it that seems to be knowable is a matter of dispute. The same can be said of the letter of James.

James has suffered from being read in various contexts that have rather dramatically affected how it has been perceived. Its position in most Greek manuscripts, after Acts, at the head of the Catholic letters, and before the letters of Paul, implied a historicizing reading, viewing it as a letter by the James who is featured in Acts 1–15, whose colleagues Peter and John also wrote letters. The arrangement found in most contemporary Bibles, where it follows Acts and Paul's genuine and spurious letters renders James, by virtue of its small size, an afterthought, easily ignored. At least since the time of Luther, James has stood in the shadow of Paul, either dismissed as a second-rate piece of writing or perhaps even a non-Christian writing that has somehow found its way into the canon.

All of the issues that have been mentioned—authorship, date, genre, contents, audience, and function—are important and deserve to be discussed. But it is important that we find the appropriate contexts in which to discuss these issues. For these discussions, the primary evidence is James, not James as it appears in later manuscripts, or James in the canon, or James in relation to Paul. Reading James as James should be our primary interest.

Further Reading and Literature Cited

Since the 1970s there has been more attention paid to James as James, rather than James in relation to Paul:

Batten, Alicia J. 2009. *What Are They Saying about the Letter of James?* WATSA. New York: Paulist.

Davids, Peter H. 1988. 'The Epistle of James in Modern Discussion'. *Aufstieg und Niedergang der römischen Welt II Principat* 25.5: 3621–45.

Hahn, Ferdinand, and Peter Müller. 1998. 'Der Jakobusbrief'. *Theologische Rundschau* 63.1: 1–73.

Niebuhr, Karl-Wilhelm. 2004. 'A New Perspective on James? Neuere Forschungen zum Jakobusbrief'. *Theologische Literaturzeitung* 129.10: 1019–44.

Niebuhr, Karl-Wilhelm. 2009. 'James in the Minds of the Recipients: A Letter from Jerusalem'. Pages 43–54 in *The Catholic Epistles and Apostolic Tradition*. Edited by K.-W. Niebuhr and R. T. Wall. Waco, TX.: Baylor University Press.

Webb, Robert L., and John S. Kloppenborg, eds. 2007. *Reading James with New Eyes*. Library of New Testament Studies 342. London and New York: T&T Clark.

Commentaries on James exist in every commentary series. Representing different eras of commentary, some of the most influential are:

Mayor, Joseph B. *The Epistle of St. James: The Greek Text with Introduction, Notes and Comments*. London: Macmillan, 1892, 1910[3].
With an introduction of almost 300 pages, Mayor's commentary is one of the most detailed and comprehensive commentaries on James, discussing not only authorship, attestation, date, provenance, and addressees, but providing also extensive analysis of James' vocabulary, grammar, and original language. It is still well worth reading.

Dibelius, Martin. 1921. *Der Brief des Jakobus*. KEK. Göttingen: Vandenhoeck & Ruprecht; – and Greeven, Heinrich. 1976. *James: A Commentary on the Epistle of James*. Translated by M. A. Williams. Hermeneia. Philadelphia, PA: Fortress.
Dibelius' commentary was originally published in German in 1921, and revised (lightly) by Greeven in 1957. It sets a benchmark for all subsequent discussions of James. The revised edition appeared in English in 1976.

Davids, Peter H. 1982. *The Epistle of James: A Commentary on the Greek Text*. The New International Greek Testament Commentary. Grand Rapids, MI: Eerdmans.
Davids traces James back to James of Jerusalem's homilies and sayings, edited by a scribe with polished Greek.

Allison, Dale C. 2013. *A Critical and Exegetical Commentary on the Epistle of James*. ICC. New York and London: Bloomsbury.
The most comprehensive recent commentary on James to date. Allison treats James as a pseudepigraphon from early second century Rome.

On the figure of James the Just in history and Christian tradition:

Myllykoski, Matti. 2006–2007. 'James the Just in History and Tradition: Perspectives of Past and Present Scholarship'. *CBR* 5.1: 72–122; 6.1: 11–98.

2

Attestation, Authorship, and Date

James is unlike many other NT writings, which were quoted or mentioned by authors in the second century CE and for which papyrus copies from the early third century are extant. Quotations of James were slow to appear in the Greek East and even slower in the Latin West. The letter was a latecomer to the NT canon, not having been included in several of the earliest canon lists. The manuscript history is equally puzzling: papyri of James are attested only in the mid-third century, a bit later than most other NT books. Latin translations of the letter appeared later, and examination of those translations suggests that the letter followed a different transmissional path in Latin than other NT books.

In antiquity persistent doubts were raised about the authoritative status of the letter and since the sixteenth century its attribution to James of Jerusalem has faced serious challenges. The dominant view now is that the letter is a pseudepigraphon. This, of course, also has implications for the date of the letter.

The Attestation of James

James is framed as a letter written by one of the most important figures of the first generation of Christ followers, James the brother of Jesus, who was executed in 62 CE. Curiously, however, references to the letter and quotations of it appear only from the third century CE onwards.

Some scholars had thought that portions of James were already cited, although not by name, in the second century, in the *Book of Thomas the Contender* (NHC II,7), 1 Clement, Hermas, and 1 Peter. This of course would mean that James was composed and available by the end of the first century CE. The *Book of Thomas the Contender*, probably from the second century, has a few convergences with James. Like Jas 1:2–8 Thomas treats desire as the threat to the pursuit of perfection (140.25; cf. Jas 1:14–15), functioning like a bit in the mouth (140.30; cf. Jas 3:3) to lead the soul astray. This hardly amounts to evidence of knowledge of James (or vice versa), however. The idea that desire is a threat to the soul was very widespread and the bit was a common as metaphor for the control of the soul, hardly unique to James and *Thomas the Contender*. In fact, Thomas and James use the metaphor of the bit differently, Thomas to illustrate something that leads the soul astray and James as a metaphor of control of the tongue to prevent it from evil.

1 Clement and James also share some distinctive vocabulary and have common themes and a few shared biblical citations. There are few points, however, at which the two writings share vocabulary in such a way that a case for literary dependence can be made convincingly. For example, at 1 Clem. 23:1–3, the author asserts that God favours those who approach him with a 'single mind' and therefore exhorts the addressees not to be 'double-minded'. James famously uses the notion of double-mindedness in 1:8 and 4:8. Yet double-mindedness for 1 Clement consists in *doubting* that God's marvels of the past could occur now. For James, however, the issue is not *doubt* but the more basic problem of a *wavering mind* or equivocation in prayer. The fact that both texts use the distinction between 'single-minded' and 'double-minded' does not help us conclude that James knew 1 Clement or vice versa, or as Allison has argued, that both knew a now-lost text, *Eldad and Modad* (Allison 2013). Hence, the similarities between 1 Clement and James do not provide a secure basis for the existence and circulation of James prior to the composition of 1 Clement.

Hermas has more extensive parallels with James but again there are no clear instances of literary borrowing in one direction or the other. Like 1 Clement, Hermas also shares vocabulary like 'single-minded' and 'double-minded' and offers extensive reflections on the vice of the latter (Mand. 9–12). Like James, Hermas depicts desire as inimical to piety (Mand. 11–12). Yet it is difficult to find points in James and Hermas at which the verbal similarities are such as to suggest literary dependence. At best it suggests that James, 1 Clement, and Hermas belong to a similar social or intellectual environment and hence use some of the same language. A case for literary dependence requires two documents to share terms or phrases that are uncommon (and hence agreements are not likely to be coincidental) or constellations of vocabulary and phrases that are difficult to explain as accidental.

It is just this kind of constellation that is found in 1 Peter and James. James and 1 Peter share a striking number of elements: (1) an address to the diaspora (Jas 1:1; 1 Pet 1:1); (2) the alliterative phrase *peirasmois poikilois* ('manifold testings') (Jas 1:2; 1 Pet 1:7); (3) the phrase 'the approval of your faith' (Jas 1:3; 1 Pet 1:7); (4) a quotation of Isa 40:6–8 (Jas 1:10–11; 1 Pet 1:24); (5) the motif of birth from the divine word (Jas 1:18; 1 Pet 1:23); (6) a quotation of Prov 3:34 (Jas 4:6; 1 Pet 5:5); and (7) an allusion to Prov 10:12 (Jas 5:20; 1 Pet 4:8). All the more striking is the fact that these elements appear in *almost the same order* in the two letters. These agreements strongly suggest some form of dependence between James and 1 Peter. The critical question is, however, which direction? Does 1 Peter know James or does James know 1 Peter? Allison's observation is convincing: James cannot be the source for 1 Peter, at least, for the quotations of Isa 40:6–8 (#4) and Prov 10:12 (#5), since in 1 Peter these quotations include elements from the Septuagint that are absent from James (Allison 2013, 69–70). This suggests strongly that James knew 1 Peter rather than vice versa.

The consequence of this conclusion is clear: James must be dated sometime *after* 1 Peter, which was composed late in the first century or early in the second. As Allison points out, while 1 Peter was cited by 2 Peter and Polycarp in the middle of the second century and used extensively by Irenaeus and Tertullian at the end of the century, none of these authors seems to have known James (Allison 2013, 69).

The earliest unequivocal attestations of James in the East are found in the Pseudo-Clementine *Letter on Virginity*, probably of Syrian provenance, and in Origen. The *Letter on Virginity*, dating to the third century and preserved only in Latin, has four verbatim citations and several possible allusions to James. Without identifying James by name, the writer twice used Jacobean phrases

(1.11.10; cf. Jas 1:5) and reproduced James's summary of true piety as 'visiting orphans and widows' (1.12.1; cf. Jas 1:27). Even more importantly, the author quoted two Jacobean texts *as scripture* (*quod dicit scriptura*): 'not many of you should be teachers' (1.11.4; Jas 3:1) and 'he who does not transgress in speech is a perfect man, able to control and subjugate his whole body' (1.11.4; cf. Jas 3:2). This leaves little doubt that the author of the *Letter on Virginity* knew James and received it as authoritative.

Origen also knew and cited James. The earliest probable citation is in his *de Principiis* 1.3.6, composed in Alexandria between 220 and 230 CE. In a paragraph in which Origen argued that knowledge of good and evil inheres in humans, he quoted several texts as scripture (*scriptura*): Rom 10:8; John 15:22; Luke 17:21; Gen 2:7; and Jas 4:17. When he cited Romans, John, Luke, and Genesis, Origen identified the sources as, respectively, Paul, 'the gospel', and Genesis. Yet curiously when he came to Jas 4:17, he failed to name his source.

The case for Origen's knowledge of James is clearer after he moved from Alexandria to Caesarea in 231 CE. Origen's commentaries on Matthew and Romans (written in the 240s) and his many sermons frequently cited the letter, usually by name. There is no doubt that by this time Origen considered the letter authoritative, for example citing Jas 5:20 as 'divine scripture' (*Hom. Lev.* 2.4) and referring to James as an 'apostle' (*Hom. Jes. Nav.* 7.1). However, in his commentary on John, written shortly after 231 CE, Origen alluded to Jas 2:26, but rather oddly referred to it as 'the letter of James that is in circulation' (*hē pheromenē Iakōbou epistolē, Comm. Jo.* 19.23).

One commentator wondered whether Origen had just discovered the letter in the library at Caesarea when he relocated there. This suggestion is precluded by the citation in *de Principiis* from a few years earlier while Origen was still in Alexandria. Yet Origen's quotation of James in *de Principiis* without naming it and the odd citation in his commentary on John might indicate that the status of James was not settled in 230 CE, at least for Origen. A few years later Dionysius of Alexandria (*c.* 200–265 CE) cited Jas 1:13— again, not by name, but nonetheless treated it as authoritative (*In Lucam* 22).

A century later in Caesarea hesitations about James remained. Eusebius personally regarded the letter as the work of James the brother of Jesus. Yet he conceded that some believed it to be spurious, evidently because most of Eusebius's predecessors failed to mention the letter at all:

> James ... is said to be the author of the first of the so-called catholic letters. But it is to be observed that this is disputed; at least, not many of the ancients have mentioned it, as is the case likewise with the epistle that bears the name of Jude, which is also one of the seven so-called catholic letters. Nevertheless, we know that these also, with the rest, have been read publicly in very many churches.
>
> (Eusebius, *Hist. eccl.* 2.23.25)

This hesitant view is reflected again in his tabulation of the authoritative writings of the New Testament: Eusebius included the four Gospels, Acts, the letters of Paul, 1 John, 1 Peter, and the Apocalypse of John as the 'acknowledged writings', but listed among the 'disputed books' 'the so-called (letter) of James', Jude, 2 Peter, and 2–3 John (Eusebius, *Hist. eccl.* 3.25.3).

James's appearance in Latin is a more complicated story. The letter was probably translated into Latin by the mid-fourth century in an Old Latin (OL) version and then later in Jerome's Vulgate (VG). The OL version is found in Codex Corbiensis, a tenth-century manuscript from France. Oddly, this codex includes no other biblical texts. It is a miscellany: an anti-heretical treatise; a tractate attributed to Tertullian on Jewish food; a Latin translation of the letter of Barnabas; and James. The quality of the OL text of James, moreover, is markedly inferior in comparison with other NT texts in the OL. This fact, combined with the fact that the OL of James was not transmitted with other NT books, contributes to the suspicion that James was not translated into Latin along with other books, but was instead a private and rather idiosyncratic translation. In the fifth century Cassiadorus, who otherwise tended to quote from the OL, preferred the superior Vulgate translation for James. Augustine (*Retractiones* 2.32) complained of the poor quality of the OL in his comments on James.

In 356 CE Hilary of Potiers quoted Jas 1:17 in Latin in his *de Trinitate* 4.8, which might make this the earliest citation of James in the West. Hilary composed this work, however, while he was in exile in Phrygia in the East (355–9 CE). Hilary's translation, moreover, does not agree with the OL and the Vulgate was not yet available. It is likely that he used his own translation from Greek, which it follows closely. Hence, Hilary's use of James does not really count as the earliest citation of the text in the West. That honour belongs to the late fourth century, in Ambrosiaster's *Commentarius in epistolam ad Galatas* on 5:10. Ambrosiaster also did not use the OL version preserved in Codex Corbiensis, but a text closer to a fragmentary OL version preserved in a palimpsest from the fifth or sixth century (Codex Bobienesis). In spite of the vagaries of translation, however, both Ambrosiaster and Hilary call James 'an apostle' and treated the letter as authoritative.

The stronger evidence of the acceptance of James in the West comes from Pelagius's *Expositio ad Romanos*, which he began in 405–6 CE. As Yates points out, Pelagius cited James by name and in highly abbreviated form, quoting only initial words of a phrase and then adding et cetera. This implies that his audience was already sufficiently familiar with the letter not to need full quotations. This in turn suggests that James was recognized as authoritative at least ten to fifteen years earlier, that is in the 390s (Yates 2002, 487–8).

While James might have existed in the West in Greek before mid-late fourth century, it is missing from the list of canonical texts in the Muratorian Canon (*c.* 200 CE). Nor was it quoted in Gaul by Irenaeus (*c.* 130–*c.* 202 CE), or in North Africa by either Tertullian (*c.* 155/60–after 220 CE) or Cyprian (200–258 CE). Each of these authors had extensive knowledge of NT documents. Yet James is absent.

The combined evidence of the Pseudo-Clementines, Origen, Hilary, and Ambrosiaster, and the silences of Irenaeus, Tertullian, and Cyprian suggest that James was not in wide circulation *as an authoritative document* until the early third century in the Alexandria and Syria, and as much as a century later in the West. Jonathan Yates has surmised that it was Athanasius who promoted James as canonical during one of his two exiles in the West, once in Trier (335/6 CE), and a second time in Rome (339–45 CE) (Yates 2004). This suggestion is credible. Athanasius certainly treated James as canonical, having included it in his list of canonical books in his famous festal letter of 367 CE and he quoted the letter more than twenty times in his works. Already in the 340s, while Athanasius was in exile in Rome, he used James in his 'Speeches against the Arians' (written in Greek). Athanasius's use of James at this time might have been the stimulus to translate the letter into Latin (even if that translation was not of very high quality).

The Manuscript Tradition of James

Since the late nineteenth century, excavations in Egypt have yielded papyrus copies of every writing of the New Testament except 2 Timothy, as well as copies of many other early Christian texts. These discoveries have enhanced our knowledge of the state of NT texts, in some cases advancing the earliest attestation of a book by more than one century before the fourth-century biblical codices, Sinaiticus and Vaticanus. The earliest of these papyri are fragments of all four canonical Gospels, Revelation, Hermas, the Gospel of Thomas, the Egerton Gospel, and the Gospel of Peter, all dated to the late second century or the early third. Chester Beatty II ($\mathfrak{P}^{46}$), dated to the first quarter of the third century CE, is the earliest papyrus with Pauline contents, containing all of the genuine Pauline letters (apart from Philemon) and Hebrews. A fragment of Philemon ($\mathfrak{P}^{87}$) from the mid-third century was found later.

Five papyrus fragments, none dated earlier than the third century, contain portions of James.

$\mathfrak{P}^{20}$ = P.Oxy. IX 1171: Jas 2:19–3:2; 3:3–9; 200–300 CE
$\mathfrak{P}^{23}$ = P.Oxy. X 1229: 1:10–12, 15–18; 250–300 CE
$\mathfrak{P}^{54}$ = P. Princ. 15: Jas 2:16–18; 3:2–4; V/VI CE
$\mathfrak{P}^{74}$ = P. Bodmer XVII: Jas 1:1–5:20 with many lacunae; VII CE
$\mathfrak{P}^{100}$ = P.Oxy. LXV 4449: Jas 3:13–4:4; 4:9–5:1; 200–300 CE

It is not until the fourth century that complete copies of James are extant in the large biblical codices, Codex Sinaiticus (‬‭א‬) and Codex Vaticanus (B). Thus, unless future publications from the Oxyrhynchus, Michigan, or Cologne collections of papyri yield earlier fragments of the letter of James, the earliest papyrus copies of the letter from Egypt are no earlier than the first citations of James by Origen and the *Letter on Virginity*.

The manuscript profile of James offers another anomaly. Most other NT writings are attested in the three major text streams,

'Alexandrian', 'Western', and 'Byzantine' (or 'Koine'). None of the extant copies of James, however, belongs to the 'Western' group of witnesses, which in the Gospels and Pauline letters are represented by Codex Bezae (D 05) and the Old Syriac versions, and by the quotations of such authors as Justin Martyr, Irenaeus, Tertullian, and Hippolytus. The lack of Western witnesses of James is consistent with the pattern of citations of James discussed above and confirms that the letter never circulated in the ecclesial circles that used Western texts. Or at least it was not recognized as authoritative in those circles and hence never quoted.

The consequence of the late appearance of James and the lack of Western witnesses is that its textual profile is relatively uniform, that is, without major variations among manuscripts. Five hundred seventy-nine Greek manuscripts, dating from the third to the seventeenth century CE, include James in whole or in part. The great majority of these are Byzantine in their text type and display a uniform text with relatively few variants. This is probably the result of the fact that by the time that James entered circulation as an authoritative text in the third and fourth centuries, copyists were following stricter procedures in reproducing texts.

The relative lack of variations in the text of James does not mean, however, that there are no problems with the text. There are several notorious puzzles. Owing to the relatively uniform text of James, however, these problems cannot be resolved in the usual way, by searching for a manuscript somewhere that might be supposed to preserve the original. This makes James fertile ground for conjectural emendations, that is, where an error seems to be present in *all* extant copies of a text and hence, one must resort to a conjectured reading.

The most celebrated case is Jas 4:2, 'you desire, and you do not have; you kill (*phoneuete*) and are jealous and you are not able to succeed'. It seems impossibly anticlimactic to pair murder with jealousy and specially to have jealousy *follow* murder. A solution of desperation is to punctuate the text so that 'you kill' is a sentence on its own and thus separated from 'and you are jealous, and you are not able to succeed'. But nothing in the syntax of the sentence warrants such a separation. The more plausible a solution is to follow Erasmus, who suggested that a *theta* (Θ) had fallen from the text and that the original read 'you envy (*phthoneite*) and you are jealous' (Erasmus, *Annotationes* 742). Elsewhere, envy and jealously are paired (1 Macc. 8:16) and in 3:14, 16 James places jealousy in parallel with selfish ambition. The only support that exists for this emendation is a marginal addition to a sixteenth-century manuscript (minuscule 918)—which might in fact have been inspired by Erasmus's conjecture. As many commentators after Erasmus argue, this emendation makes much better sense of the text.

There are several other points in James where serious difficulties occur, some of which may be resolved by positing a very early error that entered the textual stream and thus affected all subsequent copies. Such errors can only be solved by conjectural emendation, that is, by proposing a reading even though it is not supported by any of the 579 extant manuscripts of James (Wettlaufer 2013).

The earliest papyrus copies of James are later than the first fragments of the canonical gospels, but allowing for the imprecision of paleographical dating, approximately the same time as the first manuscripts of Philemon ($\mathfrak{P}^{87}$, 200–250 CE), 1 Timothy ($\mathfrak{P}^{133}$, third century), and Titus ($\mathfrak{P}^{32}$, 200–300 CE). Logically, if the first copies of James appear around the same time as the first copy of Philemon, universally supposed to be an authentic letter of Paul, nothing would preclude a mid-first-century date for James. Yet, the late appearance of citations of James by early Christian writers suggests either a late date of composition or that James for some reason did not circulate as an authoritative document until quite late. In any case, the profile of James's attestation is not easily harmonized with a view that the letter came from one of the most distinguished members of the first generation of Christ followers.

Indeed, the silence of James is telling. Nienhuis points out that during the second century a large number of texts that feature the figure of James are extant—the *Protoevangelium of James*, the Memoirs of Hegesippus, three Jacobean texts from Nag Hammadi (the *Apocryphon of James*, and two Apocalypses of James), and the glowing comments about James in the Gospel of Thomas—and one could add the pseudepigraphal letters *James to Quadratus* and *Peter to James*. Yet it is extraordinary that *none* of these makes any reference to the letter of James (Nienhuis 2009, 193). This is surely hard to reconcile with an early, and authentic letter of James, but much easier to imagine if the letter of James belongs to the second century, even the late second century.

Authorship and Date

In the fourth century such writers as Eusebius, Athanasius, and Jerome accepted that the letter was written by the brother of Jesus. Yet they knew that this was not a consensus view. Jerome's work on 'Illustrious Men', completed in 392–3 CE, reported that some believed it to have been penned by someone else and then published under James's name:

> James … wrote a single letter which is among the seven catholic letters; even this is claimed by some to have been published by someone else under his name, and gradually, as time went on, to have gained authority.
>
> (Jerome, *De viris illustribus* PL 23:609A–609B)

Doubts about James did not arise from knowledge that James was being used by heretics or groups of dubious orthodoxy, as was the case with the Gospel of John. Nor did the doubts come from concerns about the contents of James, which were never flagged as of dubious orthodoxy. The problem with James is that it was not in widespread circulation at all.

During the mediaeval period, James was accepted as authoritative and there were few doubts about its authorship. This all changed in the sixteenth century when doubts about the authorship of James were formulated more systematically. Erasmus had noticed that in none of the Greek manuscripts of James was James ever called an apostle and he wondered whether another James had composed the letter and that he had been confused with the apostle James, the brother of Jesus (*Annotationes*, 737). Erasmus also had stylistic grounds for doubting Jacobean authorship:

> For neither does it seem to bear anywhere that apostolic majesty and dignity, nor the large number of Hebraisms that one would expect from James, who was bishop of Jerusalem.
>
> (Erasmus, *Annotationes*, 744)

Luther's nemesis, Cardinal Thomas de Vio (Cajetan) also had his doubts:

It is not even certain whether the letter is by James the brother of the Lord. The greeting [*chairein*] is simple and agrees with no other apostolic letter whatsoever. It does not mention God or Jesus Christ or grace or peace but is a profane-type greeting; nor does he [the author] call himself an apostle but only a servant of Jesus Christ.

(Cajetan, *In omnes divi Pauli et aliorum apostolorum epistolas Commentarii*, Lyons 1531, 1639, p. 362)

Luther agreed. When in the famous debate with Luther in 1519, Johannes Eck cited Jas 2:17 ('faith without works is dead'), Luther retorted:

The style of that epistle is far beneath the apostolic majesty, nor does it compare in any way with that of Paul; now Paul speaks of living faith. Faith that is dead is not faith; it is opinion.

(Luther, *Resolutiones super propositionibus Lipsiae diputatis*, WA 2:425)

By 1522 Luther had assembled other arguments against Jacobean authorship: (1) Jas 2:14–26 contradicted Paul in Romans; (2) it did not 'proclaim Christ'—a key criterion of apostolicity for Luther; and (3) it was chaotically organized (*Preface to the Epistles of James and Jude* [1522], LW 35:362).

Most of these arguments are irrelevant to the issue of authorship. That the letter of James contradicts Paul and that it has a loose internal organization have no bearing on whether it is Jacobean or not. Erasmus and Luther's judgments that it lacks 'apostolic majesty' are impressionistic, based on assumptions about how apostolic letters *should* sound. The only argument worth considering is Erasmus's philological observation that James lacks a style in Greek that one should expect of James of Jerusalem, that is, that it does not *sound* like the composition of someone whose first language was Aramaic. Erasmus, great philologian that he was, had a point, to which I will return.

In the modern period, arguments have been mounted in favour of both Jacobean authorship and pseudepigraphy. Let us begin with the case for Jacobean authorship.

Defenses of Jacobean Authorship

1. Some argue that the author's self-identification in Jas 1:1, 'James a slave of God and of the Lord Jesus Christ' is so simple and unassuming that it must be authentic for, so the argument goes, a pseudepigrapher would surely embellish his credentials by adding 'apostle' or 'brother of Jesus', or other such claims to authority. Yet there are many pseudepigraphical letters whose epistolary prescripts are no more elaborate than James. In fact, it was quite usual in pseudepigraphal compositions to omit distinguishing titles and patronyms from the putative author's name, especially when one could assume that the readers would identify the author from the reputation that attached to the name. This is surely the case with James.

2. A second argument in favour of Jacobean authorship concerns the content of the letter. As most commentators recognize, the letter reflects largely Jewish or Jewish-Christian content, or rather, that it does not touch on the issues peculiar to the Jesus movement in largely Gentile areas: circumcision, *kashruth*, and Sabbath observance. James takes for granted the validity of the Jewish Bible as a point of departure for argumentation; he appeals to his audience with nomocentric categories (1:25; 2:8–11; 4:11–12); he employs an ethnocentric notion in his fictive addressed to the 'twelve tribes in the diaspora'; he refers to God at 5:4 as *kyrios Sabaōth*, 'the Lord Sabaoth'; and he employs the distinctive cultural trope of concern for orphans and widows (1:27; cf. Deut 14:29; Job 31:16; Ps 146:9; Isa 1:17, 23). Yet as most will recognize, none of these requires either Jacobean authorship or a Palestinian milieu. What these features suggest is that the letter addresses diaspora Judaeans and/or Christ followers who identify themselves as diaspora Judaeans and who know the Jewish Bible and prize the observance of the Torah.

3. Some have argued that the letter of James presupposes a Palestinian locale. The weakest indications are the mention of the cultivation of olives and figs (3:12) and the waves of the sea (1:6; 3:4). Olives and figs are cultivated at altitudes below 800 metres above sea level, which covers most of the Mediterranean region. If anything, the mention of the sea tells *against* an origin in Jerusalem, which is not near the sea or any other body of water. The mention of the sea would in fact allow most coastal Mediterranean locations, including as Caesarea Maritima, Tyre, Sidon, Alexandria, Antioch,

and Rome, but also Tiberias, near the Kinneret which often has high waves in the winter.

More important are James' use of *synagōgē* (2:2) for a place of assembly, instead of *proseuchē* ('prayer house'). Thus, the argument goes, James does not use a diasporic term (*proseuchē*) for a meeting place, but one that is attested in Palestine (e.g., the Theodotus synagogue inscription [CIIP I/1 9] and Josephus, *Bell.* 2.285, 289). The argument, however, is faulty. Although *proseuchē* is the preferred term for meeting places on Delos and in Jewish inscriptions from Egypt, *synagōgē* was used by Philo (*Prob.* 81) in Alexandria and it is well attested in Cyrenaica, the Bosphoros region, Asia, and in Rome. James's use of *synagōgē* cannot be used to settle the provenance of the letter.

Examples of local knowledge—that is, references that betray knowledge of local geographical or climatological facts—can sometimes provide clues about the provenance of a writing. As will be noted in Chapter 4, James refers in Jas 1:9–11, via Isa 40:6–7, to the Saharan wind that burns vegetation in the Eastern Mediterranean in the early Spring. Although this is not proof of Jacobean authorship—anyone living in the Levant would know about the *ḥamsin* wind—it may suggest an origin of the text in the East. But because this is a literary reference, one could also conclude that anyone who knew the LXX could use the burning wind as an illustration of the transience of wealth. The same argument applies to James's allusion to the early and late rains (Jas 5:7). The phrase 'the early and the late rains' became a literary trope in Jewish literature (Deut 11:14; Hos 6:3; Jer 5:24; Joel 2:23; Zech 10:1; 11QBlessings 8), and anyone who had this literature could use the phrase, irrespective of where they lived. Finally, James uses 'Gehenna' (3:6), a local term for a place of punishment that derives from the *Gē Hinnom* or the Hinnom Valley on the southern slope of Jerusalem. Unlike the examples of the burning wind and the early and late rains, 'Gehenna' is not found in the LXX and hence one cannot argue that James derived the term from the Greek Bible. The term, however, shows widespread diffusion in the literature of the early Christ movement, appearing in documents that certainly do not have a Palestinian provenance: four times in Mark and Luke, which are unlikely to be authored in Palestine; 2 Clement (Alexandria); Justin Martyr (Rome); the Acts of John; and Clement of Alexandria (Alexandria).

Hence, none of the arguments adduced in support of Jacobean authorship is particularly strong, and none is compelling.

The Case for Pseudepigraphy

Like the argument favouring Jacobean authorship, some of the arguments used in support of pseudepigraphy are not strong. The fact that there is a considerable volume of Jacobean pseudepigraphy has no bearing on whether the letter of James is itself a pseudepigraphon. The early and persistent doubts about the authenticity of the letter are perhaps red flags that invite further investigation, but they are not in themselves proof that James is a pseudepigraphon. More troubling are the facts the letter does not seem to have been quoted at all in the second century CE by authors like Irenaeus or Tertullian, who otherwise were well acquainted with the breadth of early Christian literature, and that James was not recognized as authoritative until sometime in the third century in the East and even later in the West.

The stronger reason for concluding that James is a pseudepigraphon is its level of Greek and awareness of rhetorical conventions. Assessments of James's Greek vary, but in general one should agree with Mayor's judgment that James's Greek 'approach[es] more nearly to the standard of classical purity than that of any other book of the NT with the exception perhaps of the Epistle to the Hebrews' (Mayor 1892, ccliv). There are a few lapses and usages of semitizing expressions that would sound odd to a native Greek speaker. But on the other hand, James has alliterations possible only in Greek and grammatical constructions that are impossible in Semitic languages, learned phrases, and even a line in dactylic hexameter (1:17, *pāsă dŏ|sīs ăgă|thē kaī | pān dŏ|rēmă tĕ|leīōn*, 'every gift is good, and every perfect present … ').

What makes it even more unlikely that James is of Jacobean origin is its lexical profile. James displays striking agreements with the vocabulary that appears only in the later NT writings: Luke–Acts, 1–2 Timothy, 1–2 Peter; in the later books of the LXX: *1–4 Maccabees*, Wisdom of Solomon, and Sirach; and in Philo of Alexandria. That is, James's vocabularic profile aligns with that of Hellenistic Judaism. Just as importantly, James employs a number of words that are among the *least* common words in Greek prior to the second century CE and a few of James's words have been suspect as his coinage. For example, James uses several philosophical terms that are rarely attested in six centuries of Greek literature prior to James—that is, they do not belong to the most basic tiers of Greek vocabulary. A few words appear for the first time in James, although some of them are also found in 1 Clement and Hermas.

Even more significantly, James uses vocabulary that belongs to epic and lyric registers: *age* (4:13; 5:1, 'come now!'), *bruō* (3:11, 'gush'), *damazō* (3:7, 8, 'tame'), and *enalios* (3:7, 'maritime'). This vocabulary points to a relatively sophisticated level of lexical use, which is a marker either of a native speaker with a rich vocabulary or someone with pretensions to learning.

This issue is not whether someone in Palestine could speak and read Greek. That is amply demonstrated by inscriptions and other data. Nor is it unlikely that some members of the Jerusalem Christ group could write Greek or that even that the brother of Jesus, who surely spoke Aramaic as his first language, could speak and write some Greek. The issue is whether James, from a family of artisans, could have acquired the *level of Greek* displayed in the letter of James. Second-language learners typically use the most basic tiers (or registers) of vocabulary, for example saying 'I will start a project' rather than 'I will launch a project'. Use of high-register words presupposes either an educated native speaker or a very well-trained second-language learner. The question is whether James, from a non-elite family, without access to expensive grammatical and rhetorical schools, could have acquired the facility in Greek that is evidenced in the letter of James. If the questions are framed in this way, then the answer is surely No.

Some of those who acknowledge the good quality of the Greek of the letter and yet affirm Jacobean authorship do so by arguing that he was assisted by a secretary or amanuensis. This of course tacitly admits that the brother of Jesus was incapable of such a level of composition. It is not, however, simply the level of Greek grammar and vocabulary of the letter that disallows Jacobean authorship. It has also been recognized that the content of the letter reflects Stoic conceptions of the law as a written expression of the divine law and their psychology, based on the view that desire was a threat to the balance of the soul (Jackson-McCabe 2001; Kloppenborg 2010). That is, the grammar, vocabulary, *and* contents of the letter are well beyond what one could reasonably attribute to James of Jerusalem.

This means that the letter is a pseudepigraphon, ascribed to James of Jerusalem, but composed by someone with a high level of competence in Greek and with philosophical inclinations. These are most unlikely to have been part of the world of James of Jerusalem.

Provenance and Date

Once Jacobean authorship is deemed to be unlikely, deciding the date and provenance for the letter are not simple tasks. Pseudepigraphy does not exclude the possibility that the letter might be provenanced in Palestine, but other locales are also possible: Antioch, Alexandria, or Rome. The reader will notice that there is little parity among the arguments that have been advanced in favour of each of these locales. The arguments in favour of Alexandria and Rome are heavily based on lexical similarities with documents provenanced in those locations. By contrast, the number of Greek texts from Roman Palestine is tiny, which means that the case for Jerusalem as a provenance for James must be built on other observations. Likewise, the case for Antioch depends less upon a comparison with the few documents provenanced in Syrian Antioch and more on hypothetical constructions of the circumstances in Antioch in the late first or early second century, and sparse contacts with the Dídache, often supposed to be Antiochene.

Palestine

Several factors support Jerusalem as a provenance for the letter, the strongest of which are references to Palestinian climate and flora (Davids 1999). The cultivation of olives and figs (3:12) is certainly compatible with a Palestinian locale; but these are pan-Mediterranean crops and not peculiar to Palestine. The linguistic or conceptual features of James that were invoked to undergird the claim to Jacobean authorship (above, pp. 22–23) are all compatible with composition in Palestine: the influence of Semitic syntax on James's Greek; the use of *synagōgē* rather than *proseuchē* to designate a prayer house; allusions to the *ḥamsin* wind; the reference to the 'early and latter rain' (5:7); and the use of *ge(h)enna* in 3:6 to designate a place of final punishment. Yet none of these points is probative. James's

Greek is influenced by Semitic syntax, but mainly by the language of the Septuagint. As was pointed out above, *synagōgē* is not exclusively a Palestinian term but is attested at many other Mediterranean locales. Allusions to the burning southern wind, and to the early and latter rains are *literary references* taken from the LXX; and *ge(h) enna*, though originally a Palestinian term, was adopted as a term for Hades by Christian literature at various locales in the Mediterranean. There is, in short, nothing that points exclusively or inevitably to a Palestinian locale.

Antioch (Or Syria)

The case for an Antiochene or Syrian origin of James begins with the observation that one of its first attestations is from Syria (Pseudo-Clementine *Letter on Virginity*) and indeed its first attestation as 'scripture'.

Second, the confessional practice prescribed by Jas 5:16, 'confess your sins *to one another* and pray for each other that you might be healed', is similar to the Didache, usually supposed to be from Antioch. Did. 4.14 enjoins the confession of sins in the assembly (*en ekklēsia*). By contrast, the parallel section in the Letter of Barnabas (19.12), probably from Alexandria, lacks the provision that confession should occur 'in the assembly' and the version in the Latin *Doctrina Apostolorum* (4.14) lacks the entire injunction to confess sins. The much later *Apostolic Constitutions* makes confession of sins private rather than public.

The public and individual confession of sins, however, is also attested as a practice well outside the area of Antioch. 1 Clem. 51.3 (from Rome) seems to recommend a practice of public confession of sins, adding not too subtly that refusal to do so might lead to an equally public punishment. Outside of Christian circles, public confession is attested in many Lydian and Phrygian 'confession inscriptions' dating 50–250 CE, where persons publicly recorded their misdeeds on a stele, acknowledging the god's power and seeking reconciliation with the deity.

A third argument for the Antiochene provenance of James depends on a hypothetical construction of the situation in Antioch: if Matthew was Antiochene, as many have held in the past, then the few overlaps between Matthew (or 'M' material) and James—

notably, the prohibition of oaths in Jas 5:12 and Matt 5:34—might suggest that James too was Antiochene. Yet, this prohibition of oaths is also cited by Justin Martyr (*Apol.* 16.5) in Rome.

A more sophisticated version of this argument invokes Paul, Ignatius, Matthew, and the Didache to triangulate the situation in Antioch in such a way as to make sense of Ignatius's letters, Matthew and James. For Zetterholm (2008), the issue in Antioch reflected in Galatians 2 had to do with the conditions under which non-Jews could be guests in diaspora synagogues. For Paul, holding that Gentiles had been sanctified through Christ and the Spirit (1 Cor 6:11), this allowed for commensality with Jews. For the brother of Jesus, however, idolatrous practices in which Gentile believers might still be implicated constituted a threat to the purity of the entire Jewish community. The remedy was for non-Jews to become Jews through circumcision and full adherence to the Torah. The Didache represents the mediating view: it did not expect Gentile to undergo circumcision, but it did expect them to observe the Torah 'as much as possible' (Did. 6.2). In the aftermath of the first revolt, and in his struggle with formative Judaism, Matthew stressed the Jewish identity of the community 'to such a degree that non-Jews no longer had a place in the life of the community' (Zetterholm 2008, 89). That is, Matthew agreed largely with the 'people from James' mentioned by Paul in Galatians. The letters of Ignatius of Antioch represent the opposite approach, one that repudiated Judaism altogether.

Zetterholm's scenario plausibly locates Matthew and Ignatius as contrasting responses to the situation in Antioch described by Paul in Galatians 2. The letter of James indeed seems more closely aligned with Matthew than with Ignatius. As I will argue in the final chapter, James disagrees with Paul's views in Galatians. James, however, says nothing at all about table fellowship, circumcision, or non-Jews. It is not at all obvious that James's disagreement with Paul have anything to do with the issues that were alive in Syrian Antioch.

James shares some vocabulary with 4 Maccabees and the Didache (both probably from Antioch), but there is nothing especially 'Antiochene' about most of these words. There is one possible exception. James uses the distinctive adjective *dipsychos* ('double-minded', Jas 1:8; 4:8) and the Didache and Barnabas use cognate verb *dipsycheō* ('to be double-minded', Did. 4.4; Barn. 19.5). The adjective is entirely unknown prior to James and the verb is first attested in the 'Two-Ways' sections of the Didache and Barnabas, the oldest part of those two documents.

The unknown factor is the provenance and date of the 'Two-Ways' document. It bears similarities to the 'Two Angels' section from the Manual of Discipline (1QS), which is Palestinian. 1QS, however, lacks the notion of 'double-mindedness'. There are no real signposts to assist in establishing an original locale of the 'Two-Ways' document: it might be Antiochene (with the Didache) or Alexandrian (with Barnabas). Hence, while Zetterholm's reconstruction of the situation at Antioch might *permit* us to place James there, the lexical profile of James does not offer any real impetus to do so.

Alexandria

Alexandria is a third possibility as the location of the writer of James. The considerations in favour of this locale are both historical and linguistic. In the first place, the earliest citation of James is from an Alexandrian writer, Origen, in the 220s (see above, p. 14) and three other Jacobean works were found in Egypt, the *Apocryphon of James, the First Apocalypse of James,* and *the Second Apocalypse of James.* The fact that other James pseudepigrapha came from Egypt is not evidence that James is pseudepigraphal. But the fact that these other documents that feature James assign to him an extraordinary important position might suggest that this view of James was Alexandrian. A good case can be made that the Gospel of Thomas and the Gospel of the Hebrews, both of which assign an extraordinarily prominent position to James, were penned in Egypt.

Stronger yet are the shared lexical items and metaphors that are rare or do not appear elsewhere in the New Testament, but which appear in James and in Jewish literature provenanced in Alexandria. Philo and James use the metaphor of the bit or bridle (*chalinos*) and share the very rare verb *chalinagōgeō* ('to bridle') as illustrations of a small instrument that is able to control a large and potentially dangerous animal. The metaphor of the bridle is common in the philosophical discussion of the control of the passions, perhaps influenced by Plato's *Phaedr.* 253C–257B. But it also appears in Ps-Phocylides (57) (from Alexandria), and with great regularity in

Philo in connection with the control of the emotions (Philo, *Agr.* 69, 70; *Spec.* 1.235; *Det.* 53; *Deus* 1:47; *Leg.* 3.155; *Praem.* 154). Like Jas 1:26; 3:3, Philo frequently uses this metaphor for the control of the tongue (*Mut.* 240; *Det.* 44, 174; *Her.* 110; *Abr.* 29, 191; *Spec.* 1.53, 241; *Somn.* 2.132; *Jos.* 246; *Mos.* 2.198; *Legat.* 163).

At least since Plato (*Pol.* 272–273; *Crat.* 390D) the metaphors of the pilot (*kybernētēs*) and his rudder (*pēdalion*) were used to illustrate God's relationship to the cosmos, the role of law in governing the state, and the relation of the reasoning portion of the soul to the body and especially to the passions. Philo employed these to refer to God's governance of the cosmos, to humanity's governance of animals, to the human governance of cities, and to the wise man's role as a 'pilot' in functioning as a teacher and moral example. Most importantly for our purposes, Philo used this metaphor of the wise person's control of the passions and as a metaphor for the rational direction of the body, comparable to James's argument that control of the tongue is a kind of rudder for the unruly self. A typical Philonic passage is *Leg.* 3.223–224, which combines the metaphors of the charioteer and the pilot and the fiery consequences of a soul that is out of control:

> Therefore, just as when the charioteer has control and directs the beasts with his reins, the chariot goes wherever he wants; but if they refuse to obey the reins and prevail over the charioteer, many times he is dragged off and it happens that the animals are carried by their force into a pit, and everything is carried away for ill. And, as a ship maintains its right course when the pilot (*kybernētēs*) has the rudder (*pēdalioucheō*) and it is obedient as he steers it; but the boat is upset when some contrary wind comes and waves (*klydōn*) occupy the sea; so also, when the soul, which is the charioteer or pilot (*kybernētēs*) of the soul, has control over the entire beast, just as a ruler has control over a city, the life of the man goes in the right direction. But when irrational feeling obtains supremacy ... the mind is set ablaze (*phlegomenos*) and burned, with the senses raising the flame (*phloga*) and throwing in objects of the senses as fuel.
>
> (Philo, *Leg.* 3.223–224)

Noteworthy here is not only the use of the bridle, the pilot, and the rudder as metaphors, but also the description of the fiery

consequences of lack of control, elements that Jas 3:2–6 shares
with Philo:

> If someone does not stumble in what they say, this is a perfect
> man, able to bridle (*chalinagōgeō*) even the entire body. [3] If we
> put bridles (*chalinoi*) on horses' mouths so that they might obey
> us, we also change the course of their whole bodies. [4] Look also
> at boats: being so large and driven by hard winds, their courses
> are altered by the smallest rudder (*pēdalion*), whence the impulse
> of the pilot desires. [5] So also the tongue: it is a small member
> and boasts great things. See what great a fire consumes much
> matter; [6] and the tongue is also a fire, a world of iniquity; the
> tongue, which stains the whole body, is set among our members,
> and sets ablaze (*phlogizousa*) the wheel of birth and is set ablaze
> (*phlogizomenē*) by Gehenna.

James's use of terms that also appear in Philo of course is not
an infallible index of the Alexandrian provenance of the letter.
The uses of equestrian and nautical metaphors in the discussion of
psychagogy and the control of the passions or tongue are found in
Plato (*Phaedr.* 253C–257B; Plato, *Leg.* 701C), popular in Alexandria
but certainly not restricted to that city. The verb *chalinagōgeō* ('to
bridle') occurs for the first time in Greek in Philo (*Opif.* 86), but it
is also found in Hermas (Mand. 12.1), from Rome.

Were it the case that the configuration of metaphors in James
and Philo and Ps-Phocylides were unattested elsewhere, a strong
case for an Alexandrian provenance might be built. But Hermas,
with its Roman provenance complicates the picture.

The fact that James is first attested in Alexandria and that it
shares lexical items with Philo and Ps-Phocylides are compatible
with an Alexandrian provenance for James. The question remains,
are there considerations that suggest another provenance, and if so,
how to account for James's use of vocabulary known to have been
used in Alexandria.

Rome

Finally, Rome has been defended as the place of origin for James. As
is usual, some of the arguments adduced for this locale are scarcely
probative.

James's use of *synagōgē* is sometimes adduced as an indication of Roman provenance since both inscriptional evidence and literary references from Rome. But as has been noted above, *synagōgē* is hardly a term unique to Rome.

It has been common to suppose that James's description of the 'man with gold rings and distinguished clothing' in Jas 2:2 deliberately invokes the specter of a member of the Roman equestrian nobility entering the assembly (Mayor 1892, 82–83; Laws 1980, 101–102). Equestrians were entitled to wear a gold ring (*anulus aureus*) and a garment with a narrow purple stripe (*tunica angusticlavia*). They could certainly be seen in Rome. Men of equestrian rank, however, were not restricted to Rome: the governor of Egypt was always an equestrian praefect. Moreover, gold rings as a sign of status can be found beyond the equestrian order, even if, as I think, Jas 2:2 means to invoke the image of an equestrian. In any event, 'gold-ringed men' in fine clothing were hardly exclusive to Rome.

I have already noted that James likely knew and used 1 Peter, provenanced in Rome. This of course does not settle the locale of James any more than Matthew and Luke's use of Mark decides the provenance of those two gospels. The main topics of the two letters diverge almost completely. James lacks to the strong christocentric orientation of 1 Peter, pays little attention to the issue of behaviour vis à vis outsiders, and lacks the Petrine household codes. On the other hand, 1 Peter says nothing about deference to the rich, the relation of faith and works, control of the tongue, or the topic of envy. That is, James may have known 1 Peter, but James has gone his own way.

More compelling is the significant number of lexical items that James shares with both 1 Clement and Hermas: (a) The much-discussed term *dipsychos* ('double-minded') appears neither in the LXX nor in Philo nor in any early Christian writing except James, Hermas, 1 Clement, and 2 Clement. Those who believed that the letter was authored by James of Jerusalem sometimes held that the work was James's coinage. But once James is acknowledged as a pseudepigraphon, Jas 1:8 is no longer the earliest occurrence of the word. The term appears in two quotations in 1 Clem. 23.3–4 and 2 Clem. 11.2–3, both attributed to a document variously called a 'scripture' or 'prophetic discourse' and named by Hermas as the now-lost apocryphon, *Eldad and Modad* (Vis. 2.3.4). Hermas appears to have made extensive use of this apocryphon, using the adjective 'double-minded' twenty times, the verb 'to be double-minded' twenty-one times, and noun 'double-mindedness' seventeen times. Twice he calls the double-minded 'wretched' (*talaipōroi*) (Vis. 3.7.1; Sim. 1.1.3), a combination of terms also found in Jas 4:8–9:

> Cleanse your hands, sinners, and purify your hearts, you double-minded (*dipsychoi*). Lament (*talaipōrēsate*) and mourn and cry.

This alignment of James with special vocabulary that is provenanced in Rome appears as a strong indication of a Roman provenance for James.

(b) James also shares with Hermas the claim that the double-minded person is 'unstable' (*akatastatos, akatastasia, akatastateō*, Jas 1:8; Hermas, Sim. 6.3.4–5; cf. 1 Clem. 3.2; 14.1; 43.6; 2 Clem. 11.4). This is a term that belongs to the lexicon of Stoic conceptions of the self, according to which the soul or mind that allows itself to be acted upon by false beliefs or desires is 'unstable' or 'fluttering' (Diogenes Laertius 7.110).

(c) There are a tantalizing number of other words that rarely appear in other NT documents, but which are found in 1 Peter, Hermas, and 1 Clement, all from Rome:

alazoneia, 'pretension': Jas 4:16; 2 Macc. 9:8; 15:6; 4 Macc. 1:26; 2:15; 8:19; 1 Clem. 13.1; 14.1; 16.2; 21.5; 35.5; Hermas, Mand. 6.2.5; 8.1.8; Philo 33×.

dipsychos, 'double-minded' (adj.): Jas 1:8; 4:8; 1 Clem. 11.2; 23.2; 2 Clem. 11.2; Hermas (20×); *dipsycheō* (verb): Hermas 21×; *dipsychia* (noun): Hermas 17×.

haplōs, 'single-mindedly' (adv.) Jas 1:5; *haplos* (adj.): 2 Clem. 2.2; Hermas, Mand. 2.1.4; 2.1.6; 2.1.7; cf. Philo 20×; *T.Sim.* 4.

epilēsmonē, 'forgetting': Jas 1:25; 1 Clem. 35.11; 46.7; Hermas, Vis. 3.13.2; Sim. 6.2.2; 6.4.2; 6.5.3; Philo, *Mos.* 1.58.

katalaleō 'speak ill of, slander': Jas 4:11; 1 Clem. 35.8; 2 Clem. 4.3; Hermas, Mand. 2.1.2; cf. 1 Pet 2:12 3:16; Philo 5×; *Letter on Virginity* 1.11.

katēpheia, 'dejection': Jas 4:9; Hermas Vis. 1.2.3; Philo 15×.

katoikizō, cause to dwell: Jas 4:5; Hermas, Mand 3.1.1; Sim. 5.6.5; Philo *Cher.* 1.1.

marainō, waste away: Jas 1:11; Hermas, Vis. 3.11.2; Sim. 9.1.7; 9.23.1, 2; Philo 9×

polysplagchnos, 'compassionate': Jas 5:11; Hermas, Mand 4.3.5; Sim. 5.4.4; 5.7.4; not in LXX or Philo.

spiloō, 'to stain': Jas 3:6; Hermas, Sim. 9.6.4; 9.8.7; 9.26.2; not in Philo.

talaipōreō, 'to be wretched': Jas 4:9; 5:1; 1 Clem. 19.4; 23.3; 2 Clem. 11.1, 2; Hermas, Vis. 3.7.1; Sim. 1.1.3; 6.2.7; 6.3.1; Philo 3×.

tryphaō, 'to live in luxury': Jas 5:5; Hermas, Sim. 6.1.6; 6.2.6; 6.4.1, 2, 4; 6.5.3, 4; 6.5.5, 7; Philo 16x and

chalinagōgeō, 'to bridle': Jas 1:26; 3:2; Hermas, Mand. 12.1; cf. Polycarp *Phil.* 5.2, but also in Philo *Opf.* 86.

As the list above shows, not all of these terms are exclusively Roman. Some also occur in the later books of the LXX and almost all terms appear in Philo. Nevertheless, the striking overlap between James and Hermas in lexemes otherwise unattested in early Christian literature is impressive. It is certainly consistent with a Roman provenance for James.

There is, however, a serious problem with a Roman provenance for James. As I have noted above, James seems not to have circulated in the West as an authoritative text at least until the mid-fourth century and it was ignored by such Western authors as Irenaeus in Gaul, Tertullian and Cyprian in North Africa, and Justin and Hippolytus in Rome until at last it was cited by Ambrosiaster and Pelagius. It is conceivable that a text composed in Rome in the name of one of the heroes of the early Christ movement, say at the beginning of the second century, somehow remained underground for a century and a half, while it gained acceptance in the East, and that it was reintroduced into Rome by Athanasius in the second quarter of the fourth century. This scenario, however, would make the transmission history of James even more puzzling than it already is.

The other real alternate is Alexandria, since it was in Alexandria that the letter was first attested, and because of strong connections with Philonic language. If 2 Clement could be located in Alexandria— both Rome and Alexandria are the likeliest of locations—it would be possible to suggest that *Eldad and Modad* may have been an Alexandrian composition and that James knew the text there. But the provenance of 2 Clement and *Eldad and Modad* remain unclear.

Strong commercial connections existed between Rome and Alexandria that might have facilitated, for example, the diffusion of texts from Rome to Alexandria (and vice versa). Regular shipping routes connected with the grain trade and the army were likely responsible for the fact that a copy of Irenaeus's *Adversus Haereses*, composed in Lyons about 180, found its way to Oxyrhynchus in Upper Egypt only twenty years later (P.Oxy. III 405). Papyrus copies of Hermas, found in Egypt and dated to the second or third century CE, also attest the rapid movement of texts from Rome to Alexandria. Philo, moreover, spent time in Rome (38–41 CE) and it was likely due to his encounter with Roman Stoicism that his works afterward show more influence of Stoicism. There is good lexical evidence that Philo's thought had some influence on 1 Clement, which suggests some of Philo's works had arrived in Rome by the end of the first century CE.

Since the traffic between Alexandria and Rome in both directions appears to have been strong, James's affinities with documents from both locales are explicable. Given the very late appearance of the letter of James in the West, it seems better to suggest an Alexandrian provenance for James than to suppose that James was composed in Rome under Philonic influence, but remained virtually unknown there for more than a century.

Date

Once Jacobean authorship has been dismissed, there are no good anchors for dating James. Nienhuis (2009) proposed that James is a 'canon-conscious pseudepigraphon', composed as a preface to the other catholic letters. This would imply a very late-second- or early-third-century date, since it presupposes the formation of the collection of catholic letters. It is very difficult, however, to view James as either an introduction to the other six catholic letters or composed as a corrective to the Pauline corpus. As I will argue later, before Luther James was never read as if it took a position contrary to Paul nor was it ever considered to be a correction to Paul's views.

Given James's knowledge of 1 Peter, we must presume a date after the composition of 1 Peter, that is, sometime in the second century. If James were composed in Rome, access to 1 Peter would presumably not pose a problem. If James is Alexandrian, as I think more probable, one must allow time for 1 Peter to reach Alexandria. Given the regularity of traffic between Rome and Alexandria, that might not have taken very long. Since both Clement of Alexandria and Origen frequently cite 1 Peter, we must assume that it became available in Alexandria well before the end of the second century CE.

The best indication of date are the lexical affinities of James with 1 Clement and Hermas, both dated to the early to mid-second century. Hence, a date in the in the first half of second century is the best guess.

Further Reading and Literature Cited

On early citations of James and the text of James:

Aland, Kurt. 1987. *Die katholischen Briefe*. Vol. 1 of *Text und Textwert der griechischen Handschriften des Neuen Testaments*. Arbeiten zur neutestamentlichen Textforschung, 9, 10.1–2, 11. Berlin and New York: Walter de Gruyter.
　　This volume contains a collation of all of the manuscript variants of James from the 578 extant manuscripts (excluding $\mathfrak{P}^{100}$ which was unknown in 1987).
Aland, Barbara, Kurt Aland, Gerd Mink, and Klaus Wachtel, eds. 1997. *Die katholischen Briefe, Teil 1: Text; Teil 2: begleitende Materialien, 1. Lieferung: Der Jakobusbrief*. Vol. 4 of *Novum Testamentum Graecum. Editio critica maior*. Stuttgart: Deutsche Bibelgesellschaft.
　　This is the first fruit of the project of the Institut für neutestamentliche Texforschung (Münster) to produce a critical edition of the Greek text of James. It also includes a comprehensive list of quotations of James.
Mayor, Joseph B. 1892. *The Epistle of St. James: The Greek Text with Introduction, Notes and Comments*, lxvi–lxxxiv. London: Macmillan, 1910³.
　　Mayor's list of possible citations and allusion to James displays his characteristic thoroughness.
Yates, Jonathan P. 2002. 'The Canonical Significance of the Citations of James in Pelagius'. *ETL* 78.4: 482–9.
　　Yates points out that by the late fourth century James was sufficiently known (and accepted as authoritative) that Pelagius was able to cite James in a highly abbreviated form (e.g., 'as James says, "consider it all joy, brothers, et cetera"') and assume that his readers would know the entire quotation.

Wettlaufer, Ryan D. 2013. *No Longer Written: The Use of Conjectural Emendation in the Restoration of the Text of the New Testament, the Epistle of James as a Case Study.* NTTSD 44. Leiden: Brill.
The only full-length study of intractable problems in the text of James that might be resolved by conjectural emendation.

Author, Date, and Provenance

Allison, Dale C. 2013. *A Critical and Exegetical Commentary on the Epistle of James.* ICC, 3–32. New York and London: Bloomsbury.
Nienhuis, David R. 2009. 'The Letter of James as a Canon-Conscious Pseudepigraph'. Pages 183–200 in *The Catholic Epistles and Apostolic Tradition: New Perspectives on James to Jude.* Edited by K.-W. Niebuhr and R. T. Wall. Waco, TX.: Baylor University Press.

Grammar, Style, and Contents of the Letter

Davids, Peter H. 1999. 'Palestinian Traditions in the Epistle of James'. Pages 33–57 in *James the Just and Christian Origins.* Edited by B. Chilton and C. A. Evans. NovTSup 98. Leiden: E.J. Brill.
Jackson-McCabe, Matt A. 2001. *Logos and Law in the Letter of James: The Law of Nature, the Law of Moses, and the Law of Freedom.* NovTSup 100. Leiden: Brill.
Kloppenborg, John S. 2010. 'James 1:2–15 and Hellenistic Psychagogy'. *NovT* 52.1: 37–71. DOI:10.1163/004810010X12577565604134.
Kloppenborg, John S. 2021. 'The Author of James and His Lexical Profile'. Forthcoming in *Who Was James? Essays on the Letter's Authorship and Provenience Resulting from a Conference on the Occasion of Oda Wischmeyer's 75th Birthday.* Edited by E.-M. Becker, S. Luther, and S. L. Jónsson. WUNT. Tübingen: Mohr Siebeck.

On the Provenance, Historical Situation, and Transmission of James:

Davids, Peter H. 1999 (see above under Grammar, Style, and Contents of the Letter).
Davids presents impressive arguments for James as a Palestinian work.
Laws, Sophie. 1980. *A Commentary on the Epistle of James.* Black's New Testament Commentaries. London: A. & C. Black.
Laws agrees that James is a pseudepigraphon and composed in Rome.
Yates, Jonathan P. 2004. 'The Reception of James in the Latin West'. Pages 273–88 in *The Catholic Epistles and the Tradition.* Edited by J. Schlosser. BETL 176. Leuven: Peeters.
Athanasius's role in bringing James to the West in the early fourth century.

Zetterholm, Magnus. 2008. 'The Didache, Matthew, James—and Paul:
    Reconstructing Historical Developments in Antioch'. Pages 73–90
    in *Matthew, James and the* Didache: *Three Related Jewish-Christian
    Documents in Their Historical, Social and Religious Setting.* Edited by
    H. Van De Sandt and J. K. Zangenberg. Symposium Series 45. Atlanta,
    GA; Society of Biblical Literature; Leiden: Brill.
    Zetterholm offers reconstructions of the situation at Antioch in which
    James might plausibly be situated.

3

Genre and Structure

What kind of text is James? It will be recalled that Luther opined that the structure of James was 'chaotic' and that the author 'must have been some good, pious man who took a few sayings from the disciples of the apostles and thus tossed them off on paper' (LW 35:397). This judgment, as will be seen, has cast a long shadow over scholarship on James.

The principal issues in assessing the kind of text that James represents concern (a) whether it is 'really' a letter as the prescript suggests; (b) whether it can be identified with any ancient literary genre (or is, following Luther, an unliterary and disorganized agglomeration of sayings); and (c) whether internally it displays a coherent structure and whether there are identifiable rhetorical structures.

Genre and Letter Form

The first two issues are intertwined. James has a letter opening, in fact displaying a form entirely typical of a Hellenistic letter, '*x* to *y*, greetings (*chairein*)', attested in hundreds of papyrus letters. James, however, lacks other details typical of private letters: a prayer for health immediately after the epistolary prescript; the personal greetings found at the end of some papyrus letters; and the nearly ubiquitous letter closing, 'goodbye' (*errōso*). Private letters also often recall prior communication between the sender and the recipient ('as I earlier wrote you' or 'as you wrote me') and have common letter formulae such as 'as you know', 'I want you to

know', and 'now concerning' (*peri de*) introducing a new topic or
an answer to a request. None of these is present in James. Readers
will recall that most of these features can be found in Paul's letters.

Because of what James lacks, some have concluded that James is
not a real letter at all, some even suggesting that the prescript (1:1)
was a later addition, giving an essay or sermon the appearance of
a letter. Harnack argued that James was assembled from bits of
tradition sometime before the middle of the second century, but
it was not framed *as a letter* much before the end of that century
(1897–1904, 1:487–490). He based the first part of his thesis on
the similarities between James and Hermas (composed in the mid-
second century)—suggesting a compositional date about the same
time—and the second part on the fact that James was seemingly
unknown before the beginning of the third century—which in
Harnack's view pointed to a late addition of 1:1. A century later
Llewelyn (1997) also concluded that 1:1 was a later addition and
observed that without the epistolary prescript, the document would
have looked like a collection of sayings of a sage similar to the
Gospel of Thomas or Q. In 1930 Windisch offered a slight variation
on Harnack's thesis, speculating that if one excised *chairein*, the
only the epistolary elements in 1:1, James might well have begun,
'the *teaching* (*didachē*) of James to the twelve tribes that are in the
diaspora' (Windisch 1930, 3–4).

Few have followed Harnack, Windisch, or Llewelyn in considering
some or all of 1:1 as an interpolation, but many nevertheless judge
James not to be a 'real' letter. Dibelius (1921/1976, 2–3), for
example, refused to treat 1:1 as an addition but agreed that James
was not a real letter. The pseudepigrapher had simply attached the
name 'James' to give the document the aura of authority.

Those who are disinclined to view James as a letter often seek
other generic designations. These include a rather wide variety of
genres and pseudo-genres: diatribe; protreptic wisdom speech;
didactic diaspora letter; wisdom text; wisdom-prophecy; sermon;
collection of catechetical material; and midrash.

Several of these are not genres at all. Without doubt, James
includes material that should be classified as sapiential, but 'wisdom'
is too broad a term to be useful, since wisdom speech is found in
a variety of sapiential genres including collections of proverbs and
exhortations, disputes and dialogues, and instructions. James is not
especially like any of these. James might have parallels in content

with midrashic literature, but James hardly takes the form of either homiletic or haggadic midrashim, both of which typically begin each unit with a lemma text from the Hebrew Bible. Diatribes use an imaginary debate with an interlocutor (cf. Jas 2:18, 'but someone will say') or a series of short questions (e.g., Jas 5:13). James, however, has far more imperatives and abstract substantives than typical diatribes, while the imaginary interlocutor only appears in 2:14–26. The use of a hypothetical interlocutor is found in other genres besides diatribes.

Before dispensing with the designation of James as a letter, it is important to consider the letter form of James again and to compare James not only with one type of letter—the private letter—but with other letter forms. James indeed lacks the epistolary features typical of private letters, but these too are often missing in paraenetic or moral epistles. The letter of (Ps-) Isocrates to Demonicus begins simply, 'Isocrates to Demonicus'. It lacks other epistolary formulae, even the initial *chairein* and the closing *errōso*. After a brief introduction, the author lists the practices by which Demonicus can make 'the most progress toward virtue and win the highest repute in the eyes of all other men' (12) and continues with a series of imperatives: 'show piety towards the god', 'honour divine powers', and 'treat your parents as you would have your children treat you' (13–14). The address throughout is in second-person singular imperatives. The same is true of Isocrates's letter to Nicocles, with contents pertaining to how the ruler should conduct himself.

Seneca's letters to Lucilius begin with 'Seneca to Lucilius greetings' and end simply with 'farewell'. These letters lack most of the other epistolary formulae found in private letters or in Paul's letters. In spite of the absence of epistolary features, however, these letters are not simply essays packaged as letters; they are letters of moral advice addressed to Lucilius ('I admonish you', *te admoneo*, 5.1); they have frequent vocatives, 'my dear Lucilius' (e.g., 1.1, 3, 9; 5.7; 6.1; 8.2; 16.1; 18.12, 15); and they are replete with imperatives: 'act, my dear Lucilius' (*ita fac, mi Lucili*, 1:1, 2); 'persuade yourself' (*persuade tibi*, 1.1); 'persevere' (*persevera*, 4.1); 'examine your hopes and fears' (*spem ac metum examina*, 13.13); 'choose a guide' (*elege audiutorem*, 52.9), etc. There is no reason to reject the generic designation of 'letter' for either the letters to Demonicus and Nicocles, or Seneca's letters to Lucilius simply because they lack the features found in private letters on papyrus.

Nor is there reason to deny that James is a letter. James is framed as a letter; it is dominated by imperatives interspersed with the vocative 'my (beloved) brothers' (*adelphoi mou agapētoi*, 1:2, 16, 19; 2:1, 14; 3:1, 10, 12; 4:11; 5:7, 12). Its contents are the expression of the traditional ethical values of Hellenized Judaism, and it invokes the moral examples of Abraham, Rahab, Job, Elijah, and James himself to undergird its advice. When one compares James with private papyrus letters, it seems defective; but when it is placed in the company of paraenetic or moral epistles, James looks like a typical example of the genre of epistolary paraenesis (see Malherbe 1992/2014).

Paraenesis and Paraenetic Letters

When Dibelius rejected the designation of James as a letter, he proposed instead 'paraenesis' as its genre. Paraenesis, according to Dibelius, had three characteristics: it was moral exhortation (and hence dominated by the imperative voice); it was typically eclectic and unoriginal in content; and it was disjointed in form—admonitions, often bits of traditional wisdom, strung together with little regard to continuity of thought (1921/1976, 2–5). James indeed is dominated by imperatives: there are fifty-four imperatives in 108 verses. Since he looked to Isocrates as his primary examples of paraenesis, Dibelius assumed that paraenesis was typically 'unoriginal' and traditional in content. This might be true of the paraenetic sections Tobit or the Testaments of the Twelve Patriarchs. But it is hardly true of Seneca's *Epistulae morales*, which are usually treated as philosophical paraenesis. Dibelius also exaggerated the disjointed character of paraenesis: as I will show later, neither of Isocrates's letters is a chaotic collection of imperatives. Nor are the paraenetic sections of the Testaments of the Twelve Patriarchs chaotic in structure; instead, each begins with an autobiographical account of each patriarch's life stressing his failings and sin, and the paraenetic sections that follow include exhortations that are organized around the prevention of that failing or sin. Seneca's *Epistulae morales* are topically organized around such themes as friendship, old age, the benefits of philosophy, moral progress, and diseases of the soul.

Paraenesis, moreover, is not a genre. It is a type of discourse that is found in several genres, including testaments (e.g., the Testaments of the Twelve Patriarchs), biography (e.g., Tobit 4:3–21; 12:6–11), didactic poetry (Ps-Phocylides), and letters, including James and Paul's letters (1 Thess 4:1–5:26; Rom 12–14). Three texts from Qumran (4QInstruction[A,B,C]) are paraenetic in content, but owing to their fragmentary state of preservation it is impossible to determine whether they were framed as testaments or instructions or some other genre. Both the Teachings of Silvanus from the Nag Hammadi codices (NHC VII, 4) and the Sentences of Sextus, a collection of *gnōmai*, are examples of Christian paraenetic instructions.

The main characteristic of paraenesis is moral exhortation addressed to an individual or group, exhortations about behaviour—what is to be done and what is to be avoided. It can draw on traditional systems of ethics—that is, traditional in relation to the particular cultural context in which exhortations are made, as is the case with (Ps-)Isocrates *To Demonicus*, which stresses such conventional virtues as piety toward the gods, respect for parents, training of the body and mind, and avoiding what is shameful. Other forms of paraenesis, however, Seneca's *Epistulae morales* for example, are examples of Stoic paraenesis which privileges such philosophical values as control of the self, hardly traditional *topoi*.

There have been efforts, both in antiquity and in modern scholarship, to further refine types of hortatory speech by distinguishing advice (*symbouleutikos logos*), exhortation (*paraklēsis, paraenesis*), and persuasion (*protreptic*). And within paraenesis, some propose a distinction between traditional paraenesis and philosophical paraenesis. Such efforts were far from universal, and many authors used these terms as if there were practically synonymous. (Ps-)Isocrates, for example, distinguished between protreptic, which he describes as persuasion directed to friends on specific topics such as rhetoric, and paraenesis, which was general advice (*to symbouleuein*) on how to regulate one's life (*To Demonicus* 4–5). Yet in *Nicocles or the Cyprians* Isocrates conflates exhortations (*paraineō*) on private matters and public life with protreptic (10–12). Philo, in referring to Deuteronomy, sometimes call it paraenesis (*Agr.* 84; *Spec.* 4.131; *Virt.* 163) and at other times protreptic (*Fug.* 142, 170; *Virt.* 47; *Spec.* 1.299). His main distinction is not between paraenesis and protreptic, but between laws and prohibitions on the one hand, and on the other 'those (sayings) that are in accordance with philosophical suggestions (*hypothēkai*) and exhortations (*paraeneseis*)' (*Spec.* 1.299). Hence, it is often difficult to perceive any real difference between 'exhorting' (*paraineō*, *parakleō*), and persuasion (protreptic) when ancient authors did not observe any distinction.

It might be useful, nonetheless, to distinguish protreptic from paraenesis, if only for heuristic purposes. That is, even if ancient authors sometimes used the terms indiscriminately, it might be useful *for us* to posit a distinction. According to Stowers, the difference lies in both the mode of exhortation and its intended function: protreptic uses sustained arguments in addition to individual *gnōmai* and examples in order to convince the addressee to adopt a new way of life; paraenesis consists in exhortations and reminders to persist in that way of life (Stowers 1986, 92). This distinction goes back to Clement of Alexandria, who distinguished protreptic from paraenesis. The difference had to do with phases of conversion: protreptic aimed at persuading the subject to yearn for a new life, while after conversion paraenesis promised a 'cure' for the passions by the use of precepts and advice (*Paed.* 1.1.1, 2).

Clement used conversion as the fulcrum for his distinction and in this respect is followed by Stowers, who argues that the paraenesis found in Pauline letters (Gal 5:13–6:10; Rom 12:1–15:13) is subsequent to and presupposes Paul's successful conversion activities. The distinction between the states before and after conversion, however, is hardly applicable generally. The protreptic addressed to friends mentioned by Ps-Isocrates's *To Demonicus* (3) was discourse designed to encourage the adoption of particular practice, hardly conversion to another lifestyle. The Wisdom of Solomon, which is usually treated as protreptic, is not directed at non-Jews to convert them but at Alexandrian Jews in order to consolidate and enhance their sense of Jewish identity.

A better distinction between paraenesis and protreptic rests on their respective modes of argumentation. Although protreptic may employ individual maxims, imperatives, and examples, it is above all organized arguments and not merely lists of aphorisms such as those found in the Egyptian moralizing collection, Ankhsheshonq, or Ps-Phocylides. As James Collins has pointed out in the most recent study of protreptic, protreptic goes well beyond sententious paraenesis, and includes the following key elements:

(1) *Protreptic is dialogic.* While it may not take the shape of a formal dialogue, protreptic discourse is always a hybrid discourse

which contains the voices of its competition. (2) *Protreptic is agonistic*. Protreptic discourse ... is also in a dialogue with other competing *protreptikoi logoi* and traditional discourses in the rhetorical situation of the marketplace of ideas. (3) *Protreptic is situational*. The shape and content of a protreptic discourse are determined, in large part, by the milieu of its competition and audience. A protreptic text certainly can be read in a different time and place and still produce an effect, but it is moveable because the scenario of potential conversion which it dramatizes for the reader is contextually rich .... Protreptic discourse presents situations of conflict, dispute, competing claims, and uncertain futures. (4) *Protreptic is rhetorical*. A protreptic discourse has a unique objective and persuasive means appropriate to achieving that objective with regard to a particular audience. Whatever its theoretical considerations or demonstrative powers, protreptic discourse is ultimately pragmatic and deliberative, that is, concerned with adopting a future course of action.

(Collins 2015, 17–18, emphasis original)

Is James simple paraenesis or is it protreptic? Since James uses neither *paraineō* nor *protrepō*, and since ancient authors sometimes conflated, sometimes distinguished the two, the question is perhaps moot. Much also depends upon how we assess James's forms of argument and how we conceive James's overall purpose—encouragement and consolidation of values by means of individual exhortations, or an attempt persuasion to adopt a set of understandings and (especially) practices that differ from other understandings and practices (thus Luther 2010).

James is certainly not 'conversion' literature in the sense meant by Stowers. The addressees throughout are Jews: they are 'my beloved brothers'; they can be expected to see the allusions to Lev 19:15 in 2:1, 9; they keep the 'royal law' (Lev 19:18) for which James congratulates them ('you do well', 2:8); a noble name (i.e., God's name) is 'called over them' (2:7); they believe that God is one (2:19); they call Abraham *our* father (2:21); and they are expected to know about Rahab, Elijah, and Job.

Nevertheless, James is not simply sententious wisdom but, as we will show presently, structured arguments on the topics of favouritism and the Law, deeds *versus* mere expressions of belief, control of speech, and the characteristics of the perfect life.

Opponents are never mentioned but dialogic and agonistic elements are present, especially in 2:14 ('if you say ....'), 2:16 ('if one of you says ....'), and 2:18 ('but someone will say ....'). The source of this alternate protreptic goes unnamed, but it is difficult to understand the distinction in 2:14–26 between faith and deeds as anything but an invocation of a distinction made by Paul in Galatians and Romans. In other sections of James, there are explicit criticisms of the common practices of patronage (2:1–13) and ethical practices that pay more attention to externals actions and effects than to internal dispositions (1:5–8; 3:1–12).

Both paraenesis and protreptic could use contrast to underscore their points, but comparison (*sygkrisis*) was essential in protreptic, which by definition involves a turning toward (*protrepsis*) a given lifestyle and away (*apotrepsis*) from another. The exposing of the dangers of the alternate lifestyle was just as important as positive advocacy. Express or implied *synkriseis* can be seen throughout James: in the implicit contrast between the double-minded man and the God who gives singly (*haplōs*) (1:5, 8); between the respective fates of humble man and the rich man (1:9–11); between the one who hears the word and does it, and the one who hears but does not (1:22–23); between those who honour the rich, and the rich who dishonour the poor (2:2–7); between those who rely on belief alone and those who instantiate belief in deeds (2:14–26); between the 'perfect man' (3:2) and the majority who cannot control the tongue (3:1–12); and between earthly wisdom and the wisdom from above (3:15–18).

Although Dibelius was right to designate James as paraenesis, this is not an alternate to seeing James as a letter; instead, James is an example of epistolary paraenesis, and a type of paraenesis that has already developed from a sententious style toward the formulation of structured arguments and which used the form of a letter.

James's goal is not simply to list a series of do's and don'ts. Instead, he is interested in the conditions of the soul that inhibit ethical conduct. Hence, he does not simply offer a string of imperatives enjoining the addressees to seek wisdom or to avoid anger. James is concerned with the conditions of the soul that render impossible the fulfilment of that search for wisdom—a soul that is riddled with ambivalence and equivocation, infected by desire (*epithymia*), and that seeks the wrong ends (4:3). Instead of a simple injunction against anger, James treats anger as an impediment to righteousness (1:20), preventing the subject from 'receiving' the implanted word that is able to save (1:21). Rather than simply proscribing such individual acts as incautious speech or slander, James recommends the more comprehensive goal of cultivating a soul that is able to 'tame' or 'bridle' the tongue (3:1–12). This technology, of course, results in the observance of individual ethical prescriptions, but James's exhortations are in the first place to develop a pure and stable self as an ethical subject. The section in 3:13–4:10 offers a number of diagnostics to determine whether the addressees have truly controlled their passions and display 'friendship with God', or whether they are still infected by 'disorder' (*akatastasia*, 3:8, 16; cf. 1:8). That is, while James does have advice concerning what kinds of conduct to embrace and what to avoid, his concerns are deeper and have to do with the conditions of the self that produce or block actions and deeds that are in accord to the 'wisdom from above'. This is the beginning of protreptic.

A Diasporic Letter?

Before leaving the issue of the genre of James it is necessary to return to the prescript, 'James, the slave of God and of the Lord Jesus Christ, to the twelve tribes in the diaspora, greetings'. This address is of course fictitious: the twelve tribes had not existed as such since the eighth century BCE, when ten tribes of the Northern Kingdom were either killed or deported. In this sense, the letter of James was undeliverable.

In spite of—or perhaps because of—the loss and fragmentation of Israel that resulted from deportations and exiles, the tradition of letters from the homeland to various diasporas became popular. Perhaps the earliest such letter is Elephantine letter C21 (419 BCE), written by a certain Hananiah in Jerusalem to the Jewish garrison on Elephantine in Upper Egypt. Jeremiah 29 (LXX 36) and the Epistle of Jeremiah are ostensibly written by Jeremiah to those taken into captivity in Babylon, while 2 Bar. 78–87 is attributed to Jeremiah's scribe Baruch, who writes to the nine and one-half tribes, now supposedly located across the Euphrates. 4 Bar. 6:17–25 is also ostensibly written by Baruch to Jeremiah in the Babylonian captivity. 2 Macc. 1:1–9; and 1:10–2:18 are framed as Jews in

Jerusalem writing to Jews in Egypt during the time of the Ptolemies. Finally, there are two letters in rabbinic literature, *b.Sanh.* 11b, and *y.Hag.* 2:2 [IV.A 77d], written by rabbinic authorities to Jews in the Galilee and Babylon during the imperial period.

Four of these letters are associated with Jeremiah or his scribe, Baruch, and concern, understandably enough, explanations of the exile, warnings about idolatry while in exile, and a promise of the end to exile. The Elephantine letter and the two letters in 2 Maccabees exhort Jews in Egypt to maintain festivals (2 Macc. 1:9, 18) and to remember the purification of the temple (2 Macc. 2:16). And the rabbinic letters are directions from scribal authorities in Jerusalem on halakhic matters pertaining to agriculture.

The form of James—an authority from the center writing the periphery—reflects the form of a diaspora letter. The content of James, however, does not align very well with any of these diaspora letters. The notions of diaspora, its causes, or its conditions never reappear in the letter after the initial reference to 'testing' in 1:2. It is not even obvious that the 'manifold testings' to which James refers are consequences of exile or instead the quotidian conditions of the soul that is misled by the passions. James does not treat diaspora as a place of exile or a space of punishment, nor is there any promise of return to the Land. And unlike the rabbinic letters, the tone of James is not instruction or prescription, giving orders to observe festivals or halakhic practices, but moral exhortation.

Even though James does not exhibit many of the features of other diaspora letters, it shares with those letters the fiction of authorities in Jerusalem writing to Jews elsewhere. The choice of James of Jerusalem is hardly incidental. James the brother of Jesus was an authority in Jerusalem (Gal 1:19) and one who was key in the controversy over whether Torah observance was integral to the Jesus movement. Although Paul represented the Jerusalem leaders as approving Paul's circumcision-free gospel for non-Jews (Gal 2:9–10), the appearance of 'persons from James' in Antioch and conflict about table commensality indicates that the matter was not as straightforward as Paul made out (Gal 2:12). James continued to be treated as a central authority in the Jesus movement after the Antiochene controversy. Acts 12:17 uses the phrase 'James and the brothers' as a shorthand for the Christ group in Jerusalem (see also 21:18), and in Luke's account of the 'apostolic conference' in Acts 15, James is depicted as presiding and making the decision: 'therefore

I have decided ....' (Acts 15:19). In the early second century, the Gospel of Thomas assigned to James a preeminent role:

> The disciples said to Jesus, 'We are aware that you will depart from us. Who will be our leader?' Jesus said to them, 'No matter where you come it is to James the Just that you shall go, for whose sake heaven and earth have come to exist.'
>
> (Gos. Thom. 12)

Other early Christian texts reflect a similar exalted view of James. The Gospel of the Hebrews makes James the first witness to the resurrection (Gos.Heb. 7 = Jerome, *De viris illustribus* 2). The *Apocryphon of James* (NHC I, 2) and the First and Second Apocalypses of James (NHC V, 3–4) claim special revelations for James alone. Hegesippus in the latter part of the second century depicts James as an ascetic who took a Nazirite vow and, rather incredibly, suggests that he was permitted to enter temple wearing priestly (linen) clothing (Eusebius, *Hist. eccl.* 2.23.5–6). Eusebius praises him for the excellence of his way of life (*philosophia*) and piety (*Hist. eccl.* 2.23.2).

Hence, James of Jerusalem was the optimal figure, analogous to Jeremiah or Baruch, to whom to attribute a paraenetic letter addressed to the diaspora. The exemplary way of life that he was reputed to have exhibited made him an ideal figure to promote conceptions of Torah-centered piety in Hellenistic Judaism.

Structure and Rhetoric

Paraenetic literature sometimes displayed an organization strategy that compassed the entire work. More commonly, organization can be seen at the level of shorter units of sayings, and sometimes no organization at all is apparent. The *Testaments of the Twelve Patriarchs* are divided into twelve sections, corresponding to the twelve sons of Jacob. Each testament displays a common structure, beginning with autobiographical reflections of the patriarch, followed by exhortations connected to the vices or virtues that were illustrated in the autobiography. A paraenetic text such as P.Insinger is topically organized, with chapters on the work of God, gainful work, honouring parents, the practice of moderation, and gluttony. Yet there is little overall continuity between one chapter and the next and the transitions between one unit and the next are often admonitions that are seemingly unrelated to the foregoing or following topics.

Ps-Phocylides's organization is largely topical and the discerning eye can also see that some sections are organized around biblical hypertexts. For example, Ps-Phocylides 3–14 invokes precepts from the Decalogue (Exodus 20) and the Holiness Code (Leviticus 19):

Commit not adultery nor rouse homosexual passion	Exod 20:13
Stitch not wiles together nor stain your hands with blood	Exod 20:15
Do not become unjustly rich, but live from honourable means	Exod 20:14
Be content with what you have and abstain from what is another's	Exod 20:17
Tell not lies, but speak always the truth	Exod 20:16; Lev 19:11
Honour God first and foremost, and thereafter your parents	Exod 20:3, 12
Always dispense justice and stretch not judgment for a favour	Lev 19:15b
Cast the poor not down unjustly, judge not partially	Lev 19:15b
If you judge evilly, God will judge you thereafter	Lev 19:15a
Flee false witness; arbitrate justice	Lev 19:12
Watch over a deposit, and in everything keep faith	
Give a just measure, good is an extra full measure of all things (Ps-Phocylides 3–14; ed. van der Horst 1978).	

In addition to topical organization, some collections use grammatical or rhetorical devices such as a *sorites* to organize individual precepts into smaller clusters. The *Sentences of Sextus*, for example, being with a perfect *sorites*:

A **faithful** person is a **chosen** person.
A **chosen** person is a person who **belongs to God**.
A person who **belongs to God** is one who is **worthy of God**.

Worthy of God is one who does nothing unworthy of God. So, if you are striving to be **faithful, do nothing unworthy** of God. (*Sentences of Sextus* 1–5)

In the case of other paraênetic texts—Ankhsheshonq for example—it is difficult to discern any organizing structures at the macro-level or even at the micro-level, beyond a few clusters that are collected on the basis of a common formal or grammatical feature, 'serve ... ', 'do not send ... ', 'do not hide ... ', 'do not neglect', and 'do not scorn'. Otherwise, Ankhsheshonq seems to be a rather random collection of moral exhortations.

Macro-structures in James

How does James compare? There have been a several attempts to analyze the entire contents of the letter by invoking the standard divisions of rhetorical speech: the *exordium*, which introduces the topic of the speech and is designed to secure the audience's attention and goodwill; the *narratio*, a succinct statement of the facts pertinent to the issues of the speech; the *partitio*, which provides a concise statement of the issues to be argued; the *probatio* or *confirmatio*, consisting of arguments that support the case, including deductive or inductive arguments, testimonies, and examples (either historical or invented); and the *peroratio*, a recapitulation of the speech with strong appeals to pathos (see Cicero, *Partitiones oratoriae*; *De inventione*).

For James, Lauri Thurén (1995) suggests the following divisions:

1:1–18 *Exordium*, consisting of
    1:1–4: The *exordium* proper, on perseverance and perfection, including a 'short *narratio*' (1:2b)
    1:5–11: Amplification with two examples, wisdom and money
    1:12–18: *Inclusio*: perseverance and perfection
1:19–27 *Propositio* (the main statement of argument, called the *partitio* by Cicero)
    1:19–21a: Exhortation on speech and action
    1:21b–25: Main thesis: Consistency between word and action
    1:26–27: Amplification with two examples: Speech and money

2:1–5:6 *Argumentatio* (i.e., *confirmatio)*
  2:1–26: Action/money: specific (2:1–7), general (2:8–13),
    theoretical (2:14–26)
  3:1–4:12: Speech/wisdom: theoretical (3:1–12), general
    (3:13–18), specific (4: 1–12)
  4: 13–5:6 Climax: Speech and action/money
5:7–20 *Peroratio*
  5:7–11: *Recapitulatio*: Perseverance, speech
  5: 12–20: *Conquestio* (the final appeal to the emotions of the
    audience)

There is little doubt that 2:1–26 (either subdivided as Thurén does, or divided into 2:1–13, 14–26) and 3:1–12 are coherent argumentative units. It is more difficult, however, to see other portions of James as fulfilling the functions of the *exordium*, *narratio*, *partitio*, and *peroratio*. An *exordium* typically tries to construct the reliability of the speaker—in the vocabulary of rhetoric, *ethos*—or it describes the positive characteristics of the audience (Cicero, *Inv.* §22). Yet the only possible appeal to the writer's *ethos* is his self-designation as a 'slave of God and of the Lord Jesus Christ' in 1:1 and the remainder of Thurén's *exordium* (1:2–18) raises potential issues in the addressees that are far from praiseworthy: lack of wisdom, equivocation, instability, wealth that will vanish, and contaminating desire. It is true that, as Cicero indicates, an *exordium* is unneeded in deliberative rhetoric when the audience is already well disposed to the speaker (*Part. or.* §13); but if this is the case with James, *partitio* has already begun with 1:2.

As to the *narratio*, it is difficult to regard 1:2b ('when you fall into diverse testings') as a *narratio* in any real sense. As Thurén notes (1995, 271), however, the *narratio* can be very brief or omitted entirely, especially in deliberative and epideictic speech (speeches of praise or blame) (Cicero, *Part. or.* §13).

There is also a difficulty in treating 1:19–27 as the *partitio* (Thurén calls it the *propositio*). At least for Cicero, the role of the *partitio* is to set forth the theses to be argued in a way that exemplifies brevity, completeness, and conciseness, *and not by extraneous embellishments of style* (Cicero, *Inv.* §§31–32, emphasis added). Thurén's main proposition, 'accept in meekness the implanted word', is hardly a straightforward statement of the matter to be argued; it occurs only halfway through a grammatical period (1:21). One might suppose that the main proposition is 1:22 'now you must be doers of the word and not only hearers who deceive themselves', for this seems consonant with the elaboration in 1:23–27 and is supported by 2:1–13, 2:14–26, both of which deal with acts that are consonant with James's view of the Law (understood as the 'word'). Jas 3:1–12 does not continue this argument and the issue of the Law does not return until 4:11–12. The issues raised in 4:13–17 of hybris do not seem materially related to the supposed main topic either, apart from 4:17, which returns to the issue of knowing and not doing. But then 5:1–6 moves in a different direction, against wealth. In other words, neither 1:21b nor 1:22 appears to function as a *partitio* (or *propositio*), stating the main proposition.

Finally, the role of the peroration, according to Cicero, is twofold: to sum-up the issues discussed throughout (*enumeratio*) 'arranged so as to be seen at a glance in order to refresh the memory of the audience' (*Inv.* §98), and to arouse the emotions. Cicero recommends that the vocabulary of the *peroratio* be powerful, with compounds, coinages, synonyms, and words used metaphorically, and that the syntax be asyndetic, that is, without the usual connectives between sentences (*Part. or.* §53). The latter characteristic is indeed present in the final nine verse of James (5:12–20): there are only two instances of *oun* ('therefore', 5:7, 16) and two of *de* ('but', 5:12). In contrast to other sections of James which are well-connected by coordinating particles, the sentences in 5:7–20 are mainly asyndetic:

> behold the farmer expects the valuable crop from the earth .... Be patient; strengthen your hearts .... Don't grumble against one another .... Take the example .... Behold we extol those who endure; you have heard of the endurance of Job .... Does someone suffer among you; let him pray; is someone cheerful ... ? Is someone ill among you; let him call the elders .... Elijah was a human of the same nature as us .... If someone has gone astray .... Know that the one who turns back a sinner from the error of his path ....

The point of asyndeton is to make the final appeals seem like they could be multiplied indefinitely. This technique is designed to underscore the gravity of the foregoing arguments.

On the other hand, it is difficult to see 5:12–20 as a proper summing up of the foregoing arguments, especially if one treats 1:21b or 1:22 as the main *propositio* of James; the notions of receiving the implanted word or of being doers of the word and not only hearers are missing from the peroration.

Several others have attempted to see James as a coherent rhetorical argument, each proposing different divisions of the text. And while each of these proposals has merit, none of them manages convincingly to compass the entire contents of the letter within the standard five divisions of a rhetorical speech. Each is open to the kinds of objections posed to Thurén's analysis.

Most of the other efforts to discern a coherent structure in James have turned to thematic (rather than rhetorical) analysis. One of the earliest of these was suggested by the eleventh-century commentator, Theophylactus of Ochrid, who divided the letter into ten thematic sections (*Epistola catholica sancti Jacobi apostoli*, PG 125:1133). The difficulty of this approach immediately becomes clear: his first division extends from 1:1–3:12—more than half of the letter—and the remainder of the letter is then parsed into nine sections of 4–6 verses each. The longest of these is 5:12–20, which Theophylactus simply calls 'individual *paraeneseis*'—that is, with no unifying theme. Theophylactus's outline is little more than a paraphrase of the text of James; it is hardly a satisfactory analysis of the structure of James.

In more recent times, many commentators propose elaborate outlines of the content of James, apparently to refute Dibelius's claim that 'the entire document lacks continuity in thought'. The difficulty with most of these proposals, as Bauckham sagely observed, is that even those who approach the task of discerning the overall structure of James with the very same methods arrive at different outlines. 'One suspects that something must be wrong with the goal that is being attempted' (Bauckham 1999, 61). Bauckham rightly concludes that Dibelius greatly exaggerated the supposed incoherence of paraenesis in general and James in particular, but he was right that James lacks an overall argumentative sequence. Dibelius was quite correct, however, that there were smaller units within James that displayed coherent organization.

Once we dispense with the idea that paraenesis was inherently chaotic and analyze local constructions within James, a much more sympathetic picture of James's organization emerges.

Local Structures

There is general acknowledgment that 2:1–13, 2:14–26, and 3:1–12 are identifiable argumentative units. The existence of these longer units distinguishes James from the sententious approach to paraenesis that is seen in Ankhsheshonq and Ps-Phocylides, which lack extended argumentative structures extending over several lines. The opening of James is constructed as a *sorites*, though hardly as elegant as the opening *sorites* of the *Sentences of Sextus* (1–5):

> Consider it as pure joy, my brothers, when you fall among
>   variegated **testings**,
> knowing that the **proof** of your faith produces **endurance**;
> but let **endurance** have its full effect so that you might be
>   perfect and whole, **lacking** in nothing.
> Now if someone **lacks** wisdom, let him ask it of the God who
>   gives to all simply and without reproach, and he will give it
>   to him. (Jas 1:2–5)

One of the proposals that has won a greater approval is the suggestion of Duane Watson that 2:1–13, 2:14–26, and 3:1–12 exhibit the structure of what the *Rhetorica ad Herennium* calls the 'most perfect argument' (Watson 1993a, 1993b). The *Rhetorica ad Herennium* (falsely ascribed to Cicero) asserts:

> The most complete and perfect argument, then, is that which is comprised of five parts: the proposition (*propositio*), the reason (*ratio*), the proof of the reason (*confirmatio ratonis*), the embellishment (*exornatio*), and the résumé (*conplexio*). Through the proposition we set forth summarily what we intend to prove. The reason, by means of a brief explanation subjoined, sets forth the causal basis for the proposition, establishing the truth of what we are urging. The proof of the reason corroborates, by means of additional arguments, the briefly-presented reason. Embellishment we use in order to adorn and enrich the argument, after the proof has been established. The résumé is a brief conclusion, drawing together the parts of the argument.
>
> ([Cicero], *Rhetorica ad Herennium* 2.18.28)

The proof (*confirmatio ratonis*) can include a restatement of the *ratio* in other terms, arguments from the contrary, comparisons, and examples. The unit ends with a résumé akin to the *peroratio* of a rhetorical speech (*Rhetorica ad Herennium* 4.43.56–44.56).

Watson suggests the following structure for Jas 2:1–13:

Propositio (2:1): Do not hold the faith of our Lord Jesus Christ with favouritism (*prosōpolēmpsia*). This is easily restated as a proposition: Showing favouritism is a failure to obey the law. The hypertext here is Lev 19:15, which prohibits partiality.

Ratio (2:2–4): a hypothetical *exemplum* in which favouritism is displayed in relation to two persons of unequal status. The conclusion of this scenario is that those who show such favouritism are 'judges with evil thoughts' and hence inconsistent with the nature of the divine judge.

Confirmatio rationis (2:5–7): three additional arguments prove the inappropriate nature of favouritism: God has chosen the poor to inherit the kingdom but the poor here have been dishonoured (2:5–6a); the rich drag 'you' into court (2:6b); and the rich blaspheme the honourable name given to the addressees (2:7).

Exornatio (2:8–11): two enthymemes (rhetorical syllogisms) prove that failure to observe Lev 19:15 negates a claim to observe Lev 19:18 (love of neighbour) (2:8–9). This is because the violation of one commandment negates the benefit of adhering to another, since God is the author of both commandments (2:10–11).

Conclusio (2:12–13): this takes the form of an *epicheireme* (a syllogism with both major and minor premises expressed): since for those who do not show mercy, judgment is without mercy, and since mercy triumphs over judgment, one should speak and act in accord as one who is about to be judged by the Law.

Watson finds a similar structure in 2:14–26 (1993a) and 3:1–12 (1993b):

James 2:14–26: On deeds and (mere) belief.

Propositio (2:14): What is the benefit, my brothers, if someone claims to have faith, but has no works? Is faith able to save him? The two rhetorical questions are easily restated as a proposition: Faith that has no deeds is without benefit, i.e., it cannot not save.

Ratio: (2:15–16): this takes the form of a hypothetical *exemplum*, of someone simply offering greetings to a naked or hungry brother or sister. Such a gesture is useless.

Confirmatio rationis (2:17–19): three elements: a restatement of the *propositio*; a conversation with an imaginary interlocutor; and the example of demons who believe only but are not saved.

Exornatio (2:20–25): a repetition of *propositio* and examples of Abraham and Rahab.

Conclusio (2:26): summary and restatement of the argument.

James 3:1–12: Control of Speech

Propositio (3:1a): Not many of you should be teachers.

Ratio: (3:1b): since you know that we shall receive a greater judgment.

Confirmatio rationis (3:2): beginning with a well-known proverb ('everyone stumbles'), it argues *e contrario* (from the opposite), that one who does not stumble must be perfect, able to control the tongue.

Exornatio (3:3–10a): two comparisons of the small devices that are able to control large entities, horses and boats, leading to the conclusion that the small tongue can have both a great and a negative effect. This is amplified by alluding to Gen 1:26b and the creation and taming of animals. The amplification ends with a strong appeal to the emotions (the spectre of an inferno).

Conclusio (3:10b–12): two rhetorical questions on the impossibility of opposites coming from a single source.

Watson's analysis of 2:1–13, 14–26, and 3:1–12 prompted Patrick Hartin to see the same argumentative structure in 3:13–4:10. It can be analyzed as follows:

James 3:13–4:10: The Characteristics of the Perfect life

Propositio (3:13): Demonstrate your way of life by deeds done with wisdom's meekness.

Ratio (3:14): An argument from the opposite: rivalry and ambition lead one to act against the truth.

Confirmatio rationis (3:15–18): the comparison (*sygkrisis*) of two forms of wisdom and their products.

Exornatio (4:1–6): Discord is evidence of the presence of envy (*phthonos*) and desire (*epithymia*) (4:1–2); the failure to receive anything from God is the result of asking from wrong

motifs (4:3); maxim: friendship with the world is enmity to
God (4:4); God does not inspire envy (*phthonos*); instead,
God gives gifts to the humble.

Conclusio (4:7–10): Submit to God; resist the devil; purify your
hearts you double-minded; God will exalt you.

This leaves 4:11–12 (which some commentators attach to 3:13–
4:10), 4:13–5:6 (a short discourse on hybris and the false reliance on
wealth), 5:7–11 (a short section on endurance and patience), and 5:12–
20, concluding exhortations. The argumentative structure of these final
sections is not as susceptible to the rhetorical analysis that Watson and
Hartin apply to 2:1–13, 14–26, 3:1–12, and 3:13–4:10. Nevertheless,
it is fair to say that 4:11–12, 4:13–5:6, and 5:7–11 cannot simply be
characterized as random or unconnected lists of maxims.

Conclusion

A comparison of James with Galatians or Romans is bound to
make James appear disorganized and lacking an overall organizing
argument. Yet that is to compare apples and oranges. When James is
placed in a more appropriate context, that of moral and paraenetic
letters, it is clear that James is among the *better* organized specimens
of these ancient moral letters. James indeed lacks a strong sense of
continuity from one section to the next, but that is also typical of
many paraenetic letters. At the same time, it is to be noted that in its
content James has moved far beyond the sententious nature of Ps-
Isocrates's *To Demonicus* and has formulated units of a dozen or so
sentences in length, offering four rhetorically structures arguments
and several smaller units.

Further Reading and Literature Cited

Harnack, Windisch and Llewelyn all argued that James was not
originally a letter, but a collection of sayings that had later been
prefaced to give it the appearance of a letter:

Harnack, Adolf von. 1897–1904. *Die Chronologie der Litteratur bis Irenäus
nebst Einleitenden Untersuchungen.* [The Chronology of Literature to
Irenaeus along with an Introductory Essay]. Leipzig: Hinrichs.

Llewelyn, S. R. 1997. 'The Prescript of James'. *NovT* 39.4: 385–93.
Windisch, Hans. 1930. *Die katholischen Briefe*. [The Catholic Letters]
2nd ed. HNT 4/2. Tübingen: J.C.B. Mohr [Paul Siebeck].

Dibelius's important point that James should be seen as paraenesis has been widely influential, even if his definition of paraenesis is often regarded as too restrictive:

Dibelius, Martin and Heinrich Greeven. 1921/1976. *James: A Commentary on the Epistle of James*. Translated by M. A. Williams. Hermeneia. Philadelphia, PA: Fortress Press. From Dibelius's 1921 German commentary.
Engberg-Pedersen, Troels. 2004. 'The Concept of Paraenesis'. Pages 47–72 in *Early Christian Paraenesis in Context*. Edited by J. Starr and T. Engberg-Pedersen. BZNW 125. Berlin: Walter de Gruyter.
Malherbe, Abraham J. 1992/2014. 'Hellenistic Moralists and the New Testament'. *ANRW* II.26.1: 267–333, repr. as pages 675–749 in *Light from the Gentiles: Hellenistic Philosophy and Early Christianity. Collected Essays, 1959–2012*. NovTSup, 150. Leiden: Brill, 2014.
Perdue, Leo G. 1981. 'Paraenesis and the Epistle of James'. *ZNW* 72.3/4: 241–56.
Stowers, Stanley K. 1986. *Letter Writing in Greco-Roman Antiquity*. Library of Early Christianity 5. Philadelphia, PA: Westminster.

James Collins offers the best discussion of protreptic as a species of paraenesis, and Susanne Luther treats that James is an example of protreptic:

Collins, James Henderson. 2015. *Exhortations to Philosophy: The Protreptics of Plato, Isocrates, and Aristotle*. New York: Oxford University Press.
Luther, Susanne. 2010. 'Protreptic Ethics in the Letter of James: The Potential of Figurative Language in Character Formation'. Pages 330–64 in *Moral Language in the New Testament: The Interrelatedness of Language and Ethics in Early Christian Writings*. Edited by R. Zimmermann and J. G. Van Der Watt. WUNT 2/296. Tübingen: Mohr Siebeck.

Examples of paraenetic literature:

Lichtheim, Miriam. 1983. *Late Egyptian Wisdom Literature in the International Context: A Study of Demotic Instructions*. Orbis biblicus et orientalis 52. Freiburg: Universitätsverlag; Göttingen: Vandenhoeck & Ruprecht.

van der Horst, Pieter Willem. 1978. *The Sentences of Pseudo-Phocylides: With Introduction and Commentary*. SVTP 4. Leiden: Brill.

Wilson, Walter T. 2012. *The Sentences of Sextus*. Edited by John S. Kloppenborg. Wisdom Literature from the Ancient World 1. Atlanta, GA: Society of Biblical Literature.

The rhetorical structure of James and argumentative substructures:

Bauckham, Richard J. 1999. *James: Wisdom of James, Disciple of Jesus the Sage*. New Testament Readings. London; New York: Routledge.

Elliott, John H. 1993. 'The Epistle of James in Rhetorical and Social Scientific Perspective: Holiness-Wholeness and Patterns of Replication'. *BTB* 23.2: 71–81.

Hartin, Patrick J. 2003. *James*. Sacra Pagina 14. Collegeville, MN: Michael Glazier.

Thurén, Lauri. 1995. 'Risky Rhetoric in James?' *NovT* 37: 262–84.

Watson, Duane F. 1993a. 'James 2 in Light of Greco-Roman Schemes of Argumentation'. *NTS* 39.1: 94–121.

Watson, Duane F. 1993b. 'The Rhetoric of James 3: 1–12 and a Classical Pattern of Argumentation'. *NovT* 33.1: 48–64.

4

The Fabric of James: The Jewish Bible and the Jesus Tradition

There is little doubt that the author of James was well versed in the Jewish Bible in its Greek translation, the Septuagint. Although there are only four verbatim citations of the Bible, James contains allusions to biblical texts throughout, references to the heroes of the Bible, and arguments that presuppose that the addressees knew and understood biblical stories and biblical injunctions.

Since the author identifies himself with the Jesus movement and indeed as a slave of Christ, it might seem puzzling that there are no references to events in the life of Jesus and no explicit citations of the Jesus tradition. The only possible reference to the life of Jesus is the cryptic comment in Jas 5:6, 'You condemned (and) killed the just one. He did not resist you.' Yet only a minority of modern commentators think that this refers to Jesus's death. Some suggest that it is an *ex eventu* allusion to the death of James, known widely as 'James the Just'. But the 'just one' might also be generic, akin to the just man of Wisdom 2–5, or a collective term that connotes the poor. The latter is suggested by the immediate context (Jas 5:1–5), which complains against the rich who oppress the poor.

That there are no explicit citations of Jesus's sayings is perhaps less striking, given the fact that the letters of Paul rarely cite the Jesus tradition. The only 'marked' quotations—that is, quotations that expressly acknowledge their source—are found in 1 Corinthians: 1 Cor 7:10–11, on divorce; 1 Cor 9:14, on the support for envoys of the gospel; and 1 Cor 11:23–26, the words of the Last Supper. The paraenetic portions of Romans and Galatians contain many sayings that might be echoes of sayings of Jesus (Rom 12:14, 13:7, 14:14; Gal 5:14) but are not marked as such. And there are no citations of the sayings of Jesus in Philippians, 2 Corinthians, or Philemon.

James and the Jewish Bible

Paraenetic literature typically draws upon the cultural resources of its producers and intended audiences. Hence, it is no surprise to see Greek paraenesis drawing on Homer and Hesiod, the epic poets, and the heroes of Greek history to illustrate or model its exhortations. James's cultural resources are the Jewish Bible and related documents. Only biblical figures are adduced for imitation: Abraham (2:20–24), Rahab (2:25), Job (5:11), and Elijah (5:17). Unnamed, but probably virtually present is also Solomon, who is the sage par excellence who asked (*aitein*) for wisdom (*sophia*) and received it from God (1 Kgs 3:5, 10; cf. Wis 9:4). When James assures his readers that wisdom is to be had simply by asking (*aitein*) it from God (1:5–6; 3:13), it seems likely that the figure of Solomon stands in the background (Kloppenborg 2007).

Just how many allusions there are to the Jewish Bible is a matter of disagreement. Estimates range from James Mayor's exhaustive list of possible allusions (Mayor 1892, cx–cxxiv) to a much more modest but more persuasive list offered by Allison (2013, 51–4). Irrespective of whether one accepts Mayor's list or Allison's (which I use here with slight modifications), it is clear that the fabric of James is full of biblical allusions.

The allusions to the Septuagint and other literature of second temple Judaism take various forms:

1. Quotations marked as scripture or as divine speech: Jas 2:8 (Lev 19:18); 2.11 (Exod 20.13–14 = Deut 5.17–18); 2.23 (Gen 15:6); 4:6 (Prov 3:34);
2. Allusions to biblical texts: Jas 1:9–11 (Jer 9:22–23; Isa 40:6–7); 5:4 (Deut 24:14–15; Lev 19:13; Mal 3:5; Isa 5:9);
3. Paraphrases of a biblical text: Jas 2:1, 9 (Lev 19:15); 2:19 (Deut 6:4); 3:7–8 (Gen 1:26–27); 3:13 (Hos 14:10); 3:18

(Isa 32:15–17); 4:11–12 (Lev 19:16); 5:1 (Isa 13:6; 15.2–3; 23:1, etc.); 5:5 (Jer 12:3); 5:20 (Prov 10:12);

4. Biblical motifs. Care for widows and orphans: Jas 1:27 (Exod 22:21; Deut 10:18; Isa 1:17; Sir 4:10, and *passim*); the early and late rains: 5:7 (Deut 11:14; Jer 5:24; Hos 6:3; Joel 2:23; Zech 10:1); and

5. References to figures of biblical narratives: Abraham: 2:20–25 (Gen 22:1–19); Rahab: 2:25 (Josh 2:1–22); Job (5:11); and Elijah: 5:17–19 (1 Kgs 17-18).

The references to Abraham, Rahab, Job, and Elijah obviously presuppose an audience that knows the full stories in Gen 22:1–19, Josh 2:1–22, the book of Job, and 1 Kgs 17–18, respectively, such that the author need only offer the briefest allusion to trigger the audience's memory. James, however, also triggers the hearers' memories in more subtle ways, by repeating distinctive biblical phrases (#2) and by paraphrasing biblical texts (#3), drawing on the logic of the biblical text but deploying it in a different argumentative context.

Allusions

The influence of biblical language on James's diction and syntax is noticeable at a number of points where it seems clear that James means to invoke predecessor texts, even when his point is different from that of the Jewish Bible. Jas 1:9–11 is a good example.

After a short section on seeking wisdom (1:5–7), James turns to an exhortation directed first at the humble, then the rich.

Let the humble (*tapeinos*) brother boast (*kauchastō*) in his high rank, and the rich man (*plousios*) in what humbles him, for he will pass away *like the flower of grass*. For 'the sun arose with burning wind and it *withered the grass; its flower fell off*, and the beauty of its appearance perished'. So also, the rich man will fade away in his ways.

(1:9–11)

There are plenty of maxims in the Jewish Bible that contrast rich with poor that the author could had quoted verbatim. But instead of quotation, he paraphrases. Instead of contrasting the *ptōchos* (beggar) or *penēs* (poor man) with the 'rich', James uses 'humble' (*tapeinos*). Two biblical texts seem to lie behind James's paraphrase. First, the grammatical structure of 1:9–11 mimics that of Jer 9:23–24. Jeremiah 9 is a judgment oracle that announces the ruin of Israel because of unfaithfulness. In this midst of the oracle Jeremiah turns to the elite:

> Let not the wise one boast (*mē kauchasthō*) in his wisdom,
> Let not the mighty one boast (*mē kauchasthō*) in his might,
> Let not the rich man boast (*mē kauchasthō*) in his wealth.

Their confidence cannot rely on their own resources and competences, but only in the knowledge that 'I am the Lord, doing mercy and judgment and righteousness on the earth, because this is my will' (Jer 9:24).

James adopts the syntactical structure as Jeremiah's oracle but reduces the triadic structure to a single statement about the rich. Instead of boasting in the knowledge of the divine, James turns to the respective fates of the humble and the rich. The humble should boast in his high rank (*hypsei*)—although James never explains how this comes about. His real interest is the fate of the rich man: he should boast in his humiliation. Since, however, it is hardly obvious how that humiliation might occur, James must supply an explanation.

The explanation comes from a second text, a paraphrase of Isa 40:6–7. The Hebrew had announced the end of Israel's hard service (*ṣābāh*) at the end of the Babylonian captivity. The LXX rendered this term as *tapeinōsis*, humiliation, and it is this word that undoubtedly attracted James's attention and inspired his contrast of the rich with the humble person (*tapeinos*) (Allison 2000, 47–9). Isaiah's message of hope and consolation contrasted the fickleness and impermanence of the people with the permanence and reliability of the word of God. That impermanence is then dramatically illustrated through the meteorological metaphor of the *ḥamsin* (or *sharav*) wind, a hot Saharan that affects the Eastern Mediterranean in February and March, desiccating and burning all vegetation within a few short days.

1 Pet 1:24 also invoked the Isaian metaphor of the *ḥamsin*, but there it functioned to underscore the contrast between ordinary

mortals and those who have been reborn through the enduring word of the Lord. *2 Bar.* 82.7 used the same Isaian text and in a context of post-70 Israel, declared that the Gentiles will vanish like smoke and wither like grass.

James has a different application. He applies the meteorological metaphor not to the people as a whole, but to the rich man alone. He also makes the metaphor more pungent. It is not that the grass simply dries up (with the LXX's passive *exēranthē*). His verb is active: the sun along with the desert wind withers (*exēranen*) the grass so that its looks are destroyed. It is not just wealth that will fail; it is the *rich man* who will waste away in all his undertakings. This is the highly visual specter of the loss of vigor and standing of those who possess wealth. It is not just abstract wealth that fails, but wealthy people who lose their vigor. James's exhortation thus concerns the *attitudes* that his addressees should have toward the wealthy and powerful.

This focus on the fate of certain person coheres with James's advice elsewhere regarding the appropriate attitudes that the addressees should adopt: toward the man of superior social status entering an assembly, seeking influence and recognition (2:1–13); toward those who pursue their desires and passions (4:1–6), and those who boast of their future plans (4:13–15). James's use of Isa 40:7 is part of his larger interest in psychagogy—the training of the moral self to distinguish between what is truly worth pursuing, and those ends that are ephemeral and fading and which lead to destruction.

Paraphrase and Aemulatio

Paraphrases of biblical texts (#3) are also attested in James, where a text is invoked but re-worded so as to bring it into accord with the author's purposes. This is what in rhetoric is called *recitatio* or *aemulatio*, that is, rhetorical paraphrase. *Aemulatio* drew on a predecessor text, typically presumed to be known by the audience, and redeployed it in a setting appropriate to that audience and its concerns. We might think that authors would have preferred to use verbatim quotations and indeed 'marked' quotations, since these would immediately invoke the authority of an ancient author, Homer or Hesiod. That is not the way ancient writers thought. On the contrary, *aemulatio* afforded the author the opportunity both to invoke a predecessor text known to the hearers and to reconfigure, update, and adapt it to a new rhetorical situation. For example, rather than quoting verbatim the well-known maxim from the *Iliad* (2.2.24), 'A man who is a counselor should not sleep throughout the night', Dio Chrysostom paraphrased Homer in his essay on kingship: the one who is the ruler 'ought to be just such a man as to think that he should not sleep at all the whole night, though as having no leisure for idleness' (Dio Chrysostom, *First Discourse on Kingship* 1.13; trans. LCL). Dio does not bother to mark this as a text from Homer. He substituted Attic vocabulary for archaic Homeric words and added the final clause, which has no counterpart in the *Iliad*. Yet no one who had heard the Iliad would miss Dio's paraphrase. Even if, as occurs in some cases, the paraphrase is so extensive that not a single word of the predecessor text remains, the point of *aemulatio* is recall the text and to showcase the author's skill in redeploying it (see Kloppenborg 2007). The authority of Homer stands behind Dio's words, but Dio's artistry is also on display.

Paraphrase was effected in order to redeploy a known text to fit the author's concerns. In Jas 3:1–12 the topic is control of the tongue, and in this context, James paraphrases Gen 1:26, the famous text on the creation of humans and animals:

> For the nature of beasts (*thēria*) and birds, reptiles and sea-creatures (*enalioi*) is trained (*damazetai*) and has been trained by human nature; but no one is able to train (*damasai*) the tongue of people: it is an unstable evil, full of death-bearing poison.
>
> (3:6–7)

As Dale Allison notes, the enumeration of animals in Jas 3:6 indicates that he has Gen 1:26b is in mind. In Genesis's list of animals that the man is to rule (*archō*), Genesis names fish and birds first, then domestic animals (*ktēnē*) and reptiles. James rearranges this list, grouping beasts with birds, then reptiles and sea-creatures (Allison 2013, 542–3). More importantly, in paraphrasing Genesis, James makes the enumeration more comprehensive: *ktēnē* meant sheep, goats and cattle, but James's *thēria* (beasts) include all quadrupeds. Likewise, as the class of sea-creatures, James's *enalioi* includes much more than simply fish. This paraphrase appears to be a gesture toward Greek science and its attempt to catalogue living things comprehensively. Moreover, James might have used the entirely unexceptional phrase *ta en thalassē*, 'the things in the sea' to replace 'fish'. Instead, he uses *enalioi*, which is primarily associated with the vocabulary of Homer, Pindar, Euripides, Sophocles, and Callimachus, appearing with special frequency in connection with sea-spirits associated with Poseidon. Here, James's *aemulatio* of Genesis not only aims at zoological comprehensiveness, but also reaches back to high-register epic vocabulary, that is, vocabulary associated with the classically educated.

James's interest in psychagogy emerges in his substitution of 'train' (*damazō*) for the Septuagint's *archō*, 'to rule' ('let him rule over the fish ....'). *Damazō* is also a high-register word that first appears in Homer (*Il.* 23.665; *Od.* 4.637) and is strongly associated with epic, lyric, and tragic vocabularies. Its connection with psychagogy begins with Homer's description of Odysseus, who 'trained himself' through adversity (*Od.* 4.240-250). In James's own day Dio Chrysostom used this image of Odysseus as the model for one who tamed his body in order that he might do good to those he encountered (*First Tarsic Discourse* [33] 15.4). James might simply have kept the LXX's *archō* or used other verbs for 'train' (*hēmeroō, ochmazō*) that were far more common in the Hellenistic period. But *damazō* immediately recalls Homer and the techniques of self-mastery that were built on the model of Odysseus' 'self-training'. That is James's point: training of the tongue is an essential component of self-mastery (see Kloppenborg 2021).

A second example of James's use of *aemulatio* is Jas 2:1–13 which paraphrases a text from Leviticus 19. As Luke Timothy Johnson (1982) has shown, while James quotes Leviticus only once, in 2:8, there are many allusions to and paraphrases of Leviticus 19 throughout James. Chap. 2 begins with a warning against *prosōpolēmpsia*, 'favouritism'. The noun *prosōpolēmpsia* and its cognate verb and adverb did not exist in Greek literature before the first century CE. Moreover, these words occur exclusively in Christian sources and once in the *Testament of Job* (43.13). The noun seems to be a Jewish or Jewish Christian invention based on Lev 19:15:

> You shall not render an unjust judgment; you shall not be partial (*lēmpsē prosōpon*) to the poor (*ptōchos*) or defer to the great (*dynastos*): with justice you shall judge your neighbor.

The Hebrew idiom, *nāś'ā pānîm*, literally to 'lift the face', is rendered in the LXX rather literally as *lambanō prosōpon* ('to receive the face') with the connotation 'to show favouritism'. The next step was to combine the LXX's phrase into the noun *prosōpolēmpsia*, 'favouritism'.

As a neologism, this word probably would have struck native Greek speakers as a bit odd. But readers who knew the LXX would immediately understand both what is meant and its source: Leviticus. Leviticus admonished against favouritism in a judicial context—judges favouring the wealthy. In the first century, however, *prosōpolēmpsia* was used in other contexts. Paul used it in Rom 2:11 when asserting that God did not express partiality for Jews over non-Jews; Eph 6:9 called for impartiality in the treatment of slaves; and the Letter of Polycarp 6.1 calls on the elders of Christ groups to avoid favouritism.

Commentators are divided in respect to the situation that James imagines in Jas 2:1–4. Is it a liturgical gathering where a wealthy and well-dressed man is shown deference? Or is it a judicial hearing in a Christ group where wealth and status might trump the demands of justice? Or is it a meal setting, in which rather typically those of higher status had the best places to recline and were given better food and wine, while those of lower status had to stand or sit? There are considerations in favour of each of these scenarios and each scenario has been defended by scholars. The essential point for us, however, is that the appearance of someone displaying the emblems of status and position triggered deferential and even sycophantic behaviour. This is the matter against which James inveighs.

James's use of the noun *prosōpolēmpsia* deliberately invoked Lev 19:15 and this is essential to the course of James's argument. Partiality for the rich against the poor ignores the fact that 'God has chosen those who are poor but rich in faith to inherit the kingdom' (2:5); it ignores the fact that the rich are the real enemies, hauling the addressees into court (2:6); and it ignores that the rich dishonour God's name (2:7). All this is to show why favouritism, decried by Lev 19:15, violates good sense. Then James comes to his strongest point: his hearers claim to adhere to the 'royal law', 'you shall love your neighbour as yourself', which is of course another text from Leviticus 19 (Lev 19:18). But since the Law is one and indivisible (2:10), anyone who violates Lev 19:15 by showing favouritism cannot claim to be observing Lev 19:18 either. Nor, to drive the point home, can a murderer who has never committed adultery claim to be Law-observant (2:11). If the Law is a single cloth, one tear destroys the entire fabric.

Jas 2:1–13 is an instance in which the paraphrase of the predecessor text, Lev 19:15, is nearly complete: all that remains of the LXX of Lev 19:15 is the word *ptōchos*, 'beggar'. The LXX idiom *lambanein prosōpon* has been reduced to a noun, *prosōpolēmpsia*, 'favouritism'. Yet this neologism is sufficient to trigger in the hearers the recognition that Jas 2:1–13 is constructing an argument against favouritism, based on the principle that one cannot uphold one provision of the Leviticus 19 and violate another and still claim to be Torah observant.

Quotations

Given the frequency with which James either borrows a biblical phrase to enliven his exhortations or paraphrases a text from the Jewish Bible, it might seem surprising that on four occasions he quotes from Jewish Bible verbatim: Jas 2:8 (Lev 19:18); 2:11 (Exod 20:13–14 = Deut 5:17–18); 2:23 (Gen 15:6); and 4:6 (Prov 3:34). Each of these quotations is marked as such, with the citations being introduced by a reference to the *graphē* ('scripture') or to the divine speaker. Why does James bother, when he could paraphrase?

The common denominator for at least three of these quotations is that the texts in question were also cited by Paul. In Rom 13:8–9 Paul quotes both Deut 5:17–18 and Lev 19:18, arguing that Lev 19:18 sums up the Torah:

> Owe no one anything, except to love one another; for the one who loves another has fulfilled the law. The commandments, 'You shall not commit adultery; You shall not murder; You shall not steal; You shall not covet' and any other commandment, are summed up in this commandment, 'Love your neighbor as yourself.'
>
> (Rom 13:8–9)

Of course, Paul is not advocating that Lev 19:18 is a substitute for the commandments of the Decalogue. Nor does he advocate selective adherence to the Decalogue. James, however, rejects the notion that Lev 19:18 is a summary of the Torah that subsumes all other commandments. Instead, it is one commandment among others, like Lev 19:15 on favouritism, or Lev 19:13, invoked in Jas 5:4, on withholding wages from agricultural workers or Lev 19:16, on slander, invoked in Jas 4:11–12.

Lev 19:18 might be a 'royal law', but it does not exempt the pious from observing the other commandments. Lev 19:18 is not as a summary of the Torah that subsumes all other commandments. This point becomes especially critical in light of Paul's statement in Gal 5:14, which also treats Lev 19:18 as a summary of the Torah:

> For the whole law is summed up in a single commandment, 'You shall love your neighbor as yourself.'

Earlier Paul had insisted that if a non-Jew submitted to circumcision, he would then be obliged to observe the entire law (Gal 5:3–4). James probably would have agreed: the law is indivisible. But for Paul, the point of Gal 5:3–4 is to *dissuade* the non-Jew from adopting circumcision: for in that case 'you who want to be justified by the law have cut yourselves off from Christ; you have fallen away from grace'. Submission to circumcision carries with it the requirement to observe all 613 commandments. For Paul, writing to non-Jews in Galatia, Gal 5:14 must be taken to imply that for non-Jews, what is expected is the observation of Lev 19:18; other laws of the Torah, especially circumcision, are *not* required. James never directly engages the issue of the circumcision of non-Jewish males, I think because he is, as the prescript indicates, addressing Jews who are already circumcised. But it is clear from the flow of Jas 2:1–13 that he rejects the use of Lev 19:18 as a summary of the Law if that means that other parts of the Law can be ignored. Thus, he concludes, 'so speak and act as those who are to be judged by the law of liberty', by which he means the whole law.

This also helps to explain why James cites Gen 15:6 verbatim:

> You see that trust/faith (*pistis*) works with his deeds and trust is perfected from deeds. And the scripture is fulfilled, which says, 'Now Abraham trusted God and it was reckoned to him as righteousness' and he was called a friend of God. You see that a person is justified from deeds and not only from trust.
>
> (Jas 2:22–24)

Paul, of course, had made the opposite use of Gen 15:6 in Rom 4:2–5, where he argues that Abraham was *not* justified from his deeds. Indeed:

> But for the one who does not work but has faith in him who justifies the ungodly, such faith is reckoned as righteousness.
>
> (Rom 4:5)

It is hard to imagine a more direct confrontation with the view that is taken by James in Jas 2:14–26, where he declares that trust (in God) absent of deeds is dead.

James's express citation of the three texts from the Jewish Bible is aimed at contesting a Pauline understanding of those texts. In this polemical context, it would not be sufficient to paraphrase or simply allude to the text under discussion. The argumentative point is *exegetical*—the correct understanding of the scope and intent of particular biblical texts. For that purpose, direct citation was needed.

A final point on James and the Jewish Bible. In part because James's use of the Jewish Bible is allusive—that is, paraphrastic—a few commentators supposed that James did not have direct access to the Jewish Bible but knew it only indirectly via Paul's quotations or through excerpts or popular oral traditions. This conclusion, however, assumes that verbatim citation of predecessor texts was the norm, and hence any work that rarely cited texts verbatim probably did not have direct access to those texts. This conclusion, I suggest, fails to consider that the norm in the use of predecessor texts was *not* verbatim citation, but paraphrase and allusion. James only quotes verbatim when he needs for argumentative purposes to do so. Elsewhere, paraphrase is normal. Allison is no doubt right when he says that 'every single paragraph [of James] carries forward themes at home in the Jewish Bible' (Allison 2013, 52). It is hard to avoid the conclusion that the author of James has direct knowledge of large portions of the Jewish Bible in Greek and draws of it as one of the main resources for his paraenesis.

James and the Jesus Tradition

One of the enduring puzzles about James is that while the author never directly quotes sayings of Jesus, the text is littered with phrases and sayings that bear strong resemblances to the sayings of Jesus. This is all the more striking given a late date for James, since roughly contemporary documents as 1 Clement 13.2 and the Didache (1.3-2.1) used marked sayings of Jesus and in the mid-second century, Justin Martyr cites Gospel texts extensively. Estimates of the number of allusions to the Jesus tradition range from the suggestion that virtually every one of James's 108 verses has an allusion to Jesus's sayings, to more modest assessments by Dean Deppe (1989, 231–50) and Patrick Hartin (1991, chaps. 5–6). The twenty-one parallels are most commonly cited (all from Hartin):

1. Jas 1:2: Q 6:22-23a (Mt 5:11–12a ‖ Lk 6:22–23a)	12. Jas 4:8: Mt 5:8
2. Jas 1:5, 17; 4:2c-3: Q 11:9 (Mt 7:7 ‖ Lk 11:9)	13. Jas 4:9 Q 6:21 (Mt 5:4 ‖ Lk 6:21), Lk 6:25b
3. Jas 1:22: Q 6:47-49 (Mt 7:24–27 ‖ Lk 6:47–49)	14. Jas 4:10: Q 14:11; 18:14b
4. Jas 2:5: Q 6:20b (Mt 5:3 ‖ Lk 6:20b)	15. Jas 4:11: Q 6:37–38 (Mt 7:1–2 ‖ Lk 6:37–38)
5. Jas 2:11: Mt 5:27–30	16. Jas 5:1: Lk 6:24, 25b
6. Jas 2:10: Q 16:17 (Mt 5:18 ‖ Lk 16:17)	17. Jas 5:2–3: Q 12:33b (Mt 6:20 ‖ Lk 12:33b)
7. Jas 2:13: Mt 5:7; Lk 6:36	18. Jas 5:6: Q 6:37 (Mt 7:1 ‖ Lk 6:37)
8. Jas 2:15–17: Q 6:21a (Mt 5:6 ‖ Lk 6:21a)	19. Jas 5:9: Q 6:37-38 (Mt 7:1–2 ‖ Lk 6:37–38)
9. Jas 3:12: Q 6:44 (Mt 7:16 ‖ Lk 6:44)	20. Jas 5:12: Mt 5:33-37
10. Jas 3:18: Mt 5:9; Lk 6:43	21. Jas 5:19-20: Q 17:3b (Mt 18:15 ‖ Lk 17:3b)
11. Jas 4:4b: Q 16:13 (Mt 6:24 ‖ Lk 16:13)	

Efforts to account for the parallels between James and the Jesus tradition have yielded several solutions. These range from one pole, that there are no allusions to the Jesus tradition at all, to the opposite one, that James knew and used the Gospel of Matthew extensively. Between these poles, there are a number of mediating approaches which trace the similarities between James and the Jesus tradition to the personal contact that the author (James of Jerusalem) had with his brother Jesus, or James's creative adaptation of the oral Jesus tradition, or James's use of Q.

A few scholars, noted in Chapter 3 who believed that James was a Jewish document that was only superficially Christianized, argued that the similarities between the contents of James and sayings of Jesus merely indicated that both Jesus and James were dependent upon common Jewish moral traditions. Hence, James was not alluding to the Jesus tradition at all. This view has not achieved much of a following today. Dibelius offered another version of this approach. Jas 1:1 was not a later addition to the letter and hence, James was a composition by an author who belonged to the Jesus movement. But Dibelius argued that the similarities between James and the Jesus tradition were due to their common reliance on stereotypical paraenetic topics. Since both the Jesus tradition and James were paraenesis, it is unsurprising that there would be some overlap between them. This was not evidence of James's knowledge of the Jesus tradition.

The opposite view is that James knew and used Matthew, in spite of his inexact replication of Matthew's text. The prohibition of oaths in Mt 5:33-37 and Jas 5:12 (#20) provides the strongest encouragement for this view. Yet it has also been pointed out that for a number of the overlaps between James and the Synoptics, it is Luke's version, not Matthew's, that is the closest to James.

One of the more interesting explanations was that of J. B. Mayor in his monumental commentary. Accepting that the letter was from James of Jerusalem, he supposed that James, as the brother of Jesus, had so deeply imbibed the thought and manner of speech of his brother, that he came to speak (or write) in a 'Jesus-like' style. This theory of course also required the hypothesis that the letter was authored by the brother of Jesus before James's execution in 62 CE, a hypothesis that now faces rather insuperable objections, as Chapter 2 has shown.

Richard Bauckham offered a more convincing explanation. Bauckham was skeptical about any attempt to show that James knew written sources of the Jesus tradition, whether the Gospels or Q. James undoubtedly knew the Jesus tradition in an oral form. As a wisdom teacher, however, the task of the author of James was 'to distil both traditional wisdom and his own additions to it into aphorisms of his own formulation' (1999, 36). Bauckham adduced the analogy of the relationship between Sirach and the book of Proverbs. It is obvious that Sirach knew Proverbs. Yet he never quotes Proverbs, and he reproduces phrases from Proverbs verbatim only three times in fifty-one chapters. Instead, Sirach 'transmits and develops the tradition *without simply repeating it*', even when the formulations by Proverbs were entirely unobjectionable (Bauckham 1999, 79, emphasis original). He understands James's relationship to the Jesus tradition analogously:

> [James] does not repeat [the Jesus tradition]; he is inspired by it. He creates his own wise sayings, sometimes as equivalents of specific sayings of Jesus, sometimes inspired by several sayings, sometimes encapsulating the theme of many sayings, sometimes based on points of contact between Jesus' sayings and other Jewish wisdom. The creativity and artistry of these sayings are missed when they are treated as allusions to sayings of Jesus. But the indebtedness of James' wisdom to Jesus is much greater than verbal resemblances would show.
>
> (Bauckham 1999, 82–3)

And further:

> James is not *quoting or alluding* to the saying of Jesus, but, in the manner of a wisdom sage, he is *re-expressing* the insight he has learned from Jesus' teaching.
>
> (Bauckham 1999, 91, emphasis original)

Thus, Bauckham reframes the issue whether James alludes to or cites the Jesus tradition. He does not. Instead, he is 'inspired' by it or, as we might say, uses it not as *source* but as a *resource*.

Though Bauckham adheres to the notion of Jacobean authorship, it should be observed that his model for understanding the relationship between Jesus and James does not logically require any assumptions about authorship. It works just as well in accounting for the shape of James's text whether James was dependent on oral tradition or upon an early written collection of Jesus's sayings. Sirach, of course, was dependent on the *written text* of Proverbs. What Bauckham's thesis requires is only that the sayings of Jesus, transmitted to him orally or in writing, were treated as sufficiently weighty and important to merit James making them his own.

What Bauckham describes as a process for the composition of Sirach and James is precisely what I have just described as *aemulatio*. As I have indicated above, authors in the ancient world were just as likely to paraphrase their sources as to quote them verbatim, expecting their readers and hearers both to discern the text that the author had in mind and to appreciate the appropriateness of his paraphrase. Quintilian in fact says that the duty of *aemulatio* 'is to rival and vie [*aemulatio*] with the original in the expression of the same thoughts' (*Institutes* 10.5.5). Ps-Phocylides 10, for example, paraphrases the LXX of Lev 19:15, although in a manner very different from that of Jas 2:1 (see above). Yet the Jewish hearer would hear an echo of the Jewish Bible:

Lev 19:15	Ps-Phocylides 10
You shall not render an unjust judgment; you shall not be 'receive the face' (*lēmpsē prosōpon*) of the poor (*ptōchos*) or defer to the great: with justice you shall judge (*krineis*) your neighbor.	Do not cast the poor (*penēs*) down unjustly, do not judge (*krine*) by his face (*prosōpon*).

Ps-Phocylides's paraphrase substitutes for Leviticus's term *ptōchos* (beggar) the more common word for 'poor' (*penēs*), but it preserves the use of *prosōpon* ('face') and the use of the verb 'judge'. These elements would alert the reader as to the biblical text that Ps-Phocylides had in mind. His paraphrase widens the scope of the exhortation from beggars (*ptōchoi*) to the poor in general. Moreover, Ps-Phocylides turns the sentence into dactylic hexameter. Leviticus now sounds like the poetry that was prized in learned circles.

It will be noticed that the majority of James's echoes of the Jesus tradition are from the so-called Q source, and the remaining eight (## 5, 7, 10, 16, 20) are all from the Sermon on the Mount or Sermon on the Plain. This might encourage the view that James knew the Sermon on the Mount/Sermon on the Plain from Matthew and Luke. Hartin, however, observed that James's parallels to Matthaean sayings lack those elements usually thought to be Matthew's editorial additions. This being the case, it would be difficult to imagine how James could have used Matthew's Gospel and removed all of those elements that Matthew added. For Hartin, this leaves a choice:

Only two possible explanations can be given of these similarities. Either both James and Q are dependent upon a common tradition which is reflected in these examples; or James is dependent directly on the Q tradition. The argument of this investigation supports the direct dependence of James on Q. The main reason for opting for this second possibility arises from the closeness of the language used. While no one example is capable of proving the point conclusively, all these examples taken together provide an argument from convergence. If one were to opt for the first possibility whereby James and Q are independent of each other, yet dependent upon a common tradition, one would in fact have to postulate a common tradition very similar to Q.

(Hartin 1991, 186)

To illustrate James's paraphrase of a Q text, let us look at #2, Jas 1:5–8 and 4:2c-3, and #17, Jas 5:2-3.

Jas 1:5–8, 4:2c-3 and Q 11:9–13

Jas 1:5–8 offers a paraphrase of Q 11:9–13:

If one of you lacks wisdom, let him ask (*aiteitō*) from the God who gives to all, single-mindedly (*haplōs*) and without reproach, and it will be given to him (*kai dothēsetai autō*). But let him ask in faith, disputing nothing, for whoever disputes is like the surf of the sea, blown and tossed by the wind; for let not such a person suppose that he will receive anything from the Lord— (he is) a double-minded man, unstable in all his ways.

(Jas 1:5–8)

The reverse statement appears later:

You fight and make war. You do not have because you do not ask. You ask (*aiteite*) and do not receive (*lambanete*), because you ask badly, in order that you might expend (it) on your pleasures.

(Jas 4:2c-3)

Q's version of the aphorism is triadic, with three verbs, ask, seek, and knock, followed by a statement of rather astonishing confidence:

Ask (*aiteite*) and it will be given to you (*dothēsetai*); seek and you will find; knock and (the door) will be opened to you. For everyone who asks receives (*lambanei*), and the one who seeks finds, and to the one who knocks it will be opened.

(Q 11:9–10)

The focus of Q's saying is the generosity of the divine patron. Q illustrates this by appeal to two scenarios of a father giving his children bread and fish, and then concludes:

If then, you being evil, know how to give good gifts to your children, how much more will the father from heaven give good things to those who ask him.

(Q 11:13)

The appearance of the 'ask–be given' pair in Jas 1:6, and 'ask–receive' pair in Jas 4:3 is enough for the hearers to recall Q 11:9–10. The confidence expressed by Jas 1:5, that requests will certainly be granted, reflects the extraordinary confidence of Q 11:10.

The differences between James and Q are noteworthy, however, and are fully in accord with the practice of *aemulatio*, that is, adapting a known saying to a new situation. James reduces Q's triad to the simple pair of ask–receive or ask–be given, dispensing with 'seek–find' and 'knock–open'. More importantly, whereas the focus of Q's petition is on matters of subsistence—food—for James the object of petition is *wisdom*. James's preoccupation is not so much with the object of petition as with the mental attitude of the petitioner: the petitioner cannot waver, debate, or equivocate and expect to receive anything. This emphasis on single-mindedness is underscored in two ways: by James's depiction of God as 'single-minded' (*haplōs*); and by the negative example of the 'double-minded' (*dipsychos*) person, unstable and like the waves of the sea in a storm. James's paraphrase of Q 11:9–13 reflects his interest in psychagogy and the cultivation of a soul that is single and unwavering in its commitment to what is true and good. In accord with the Stoicizing tendencies of James, passion and desire (*epithymia*) are disturbances in the human soul, causing it to waver and become unstable and occluding its perception of the Good.

Each person is tempted, being dragged off and lured away by
one's own desires (*epithymiai*); then when desire conceives, it
gives birth to sin, and when sin has run its course, it brings forth
death.

(Jas 1:14–15)

Hence, when Jas in 4:2–3 restates Q 11:9–10, he does so in a
negative form: the reason that asking does not produce results is
because the addressees 'ask badly' or wrongly, for the sake of their
own pleasures (*hēdonai*). Desire, passion, and pleasure, in James
and in Philo as in the Stoics, are diseases of the soul which inhibit
the true pursuit of the Good (more on this in Chapter 5).

The reader of James would discern that Jesus's sayings about
asking and receiving were James's resource. At the same time, the
reader would see that James has shifted the emphasis of the saying
from what the petitioner might receive to the proper attitudes that
the petitioner must have to receive anything from God. This is
psychagogy.

Jas 5:2–3 and Q 12:33–34

A more subtle example of James's emulation of the Jesus tradition
is offered by Jas 5:2–3:

Your riches rotted (*sesēpen*) and your garments are moth-eaten
(*setobrōta*); your gold and silver rusted (*katiōtai*) and their rust
(*ios*) will be a witness against you, and it will devour your flesh
like fire; you have stored up treasure (*ethēraurisate*) for the last
days!

The context of this statement is a scenario of the last days when
the evil will be punished and wail because of those punishments.
Jas 5:1 prefaces his statement with the prophetic cry to 'wail'
(*ololuzete*), which occurs in judgment oracles in Isa 13-24 and Jer
31:31. But instead of addressing the nations that are Israel's enemies
as do Isaiah and Jeremiah, James addresses the rich. Here he adapts
a saying from Q:

Do not treasure (*mē thēsaurizete*) for yourselves treasures on
earth, where moth (*sēs*) and gnawing (insect) (*brōsis*) ruin and

where robbers dig through and rob; but (*thēsaurizete*) treasure for yourselves treasures in heaven, where neither moth nor gnawing (insect) defaces and where robbers do not dig through nor rob. For where your treasure is, there will also be your heart.

(Q 12:33–34)

James's use of the verb *sēpō* ('to rot'), the compound *sēpobrōtos* ('moth-eaten'), and the verb *thesaurizō* ('to store up') are enough to trigger a memory of Q 12:33–34. *Sēpobrōtos* is extremely rare in Greek literature, appearing only in Job (once), James (once), and the Sybilline Oracles (frag. 3.26), a Jewish or Jewish-Christian polemic against the Greek gods. James's work seems to be a combination of Q's *sēs* ('moth') and *brōsis* ('gnawing insect'), designed to evoke Q.

Q and James also draw on the notion of a storehouse of virtues that can be drawn upon in the judgment. This is an idea that is already present in Tobit, who recommends almsgiving as a means to enhance one's treasury (Tobit 4:8; 12:4). Q and James, however, dramatize the folly of storing up earthly wealth, which is not only impermanent but is subject to corruption and decay.

We should observe, however, an important change in James paraphrase. Q's illustrations use the emblems of wealth in a village or town: woolen clothing that can be damaged by moths; food which insects destroy; and the goods that robbers 'dig through' and steal (Q here pictures the typical mudbrick construction of rural houses, where thieves obtain access not through the door, but by digging through the wall). James on the other hand, imagines city life, where gold and silver—that is, jewelry, in addition to clothing and food are the typical emblems of wealth and status.

There is insufficient space to examine all of the allusions to the Jewish Bible or the Jesus tradition. A fuller treatment of both kinds of allusions will confirm not only that James knew and used both the Jewish Bible and the Jesus tradition, probably some version of Q with some Matthew-leaning features such as the prohibition of oaths. In accordance with Greek rhetorical practices, James preferred rather to paraphrase than to quote. His paraphrases provide critical clues to his social locations and his interests, for in the course of paraphrase he shifted the social register of the sayings upward, to appeal to an urban audience, and he introduced his interest in the guidance of the soul (psychagogy).

Further Reading and Literature Cited

James's use of the Jewish Bible

Allison, Dale C. 2000. *Scriptural Allusions in the New Testament: Light
from the Dead Sea Scrolls*. The Dead Sea Scrolls & Christian Origins
Library. North Richland Hills, TX: BIBAL Press.

Allison, Dale C. 2013. *A Critical and Exegetical Commentary on the
Epistle of James*. ICC. New York and London: Bloomsbury.

Johnson, Luke Timothy. 1982. 'The Use of Leviticus 19 in the Letter of
James'. *JBL* 101.3: 391–401.

Kloppenborg, John S. 2007. 'Diaspora Discourse: The Construction
of *Ethos* in James'. *NTS* 53.2: 242–70. DOI: 10.1017/
S0028688507000148.

Kloppenborg, John S. 2021. 'The Author of James and His Lexical
Profile'. Forthcoming in *Who Was James? Essays on the Letter's
Authorship and Provenience Resulting from a Conference on the
Occasion of Oda Wischmeyer's 75th Birthday*. Edited by E.-M. Becker,
S. Luther, and S. L. Jónsson. WUNT. Tübingen: Mohr Siebeck.

Mayor, Joseph B. 1892. *The Epistle of St. James: The Greek Text with
Introduction, Notes and Comments*. London: Macmillan (pp. cx–
cxxiv).
  Mayor's tabulation of quotations and allusions from the Jewish Bible,
  Apocrypha, Testaments of the Twelve Patriarchs, and Philo is very
  extensive, because he used a very liberal definition of quotation and
  allusion.

Popkes, Wiard. 1999. 'James and Scripture: An Exercise in Intertextuality'.
NTS 45.2: 213–29.

James and the Jesus Tradition:

Batten, Alicia J. 2014. 'The Urbanization of Jesus Traditions in James'.
Pages 78–96 in *James, 1 & 2 Peter and the Early Jesus Tradition*.
Edited by A. Batten and J. S. Kloppenborg. LNTS 478. London and
New York: Bloomsbury T&T Clark.

Bauckham, Richard J. 1999. *James: Wisdom of James, Disciple of Jesus
the Sage*. New Testament Readings. London and New York: Routledge.

Deppe, Dean B. 1989. 'The Sayings of Jesus in the Epistle of James'.
Thesis (D.Th.), Free University of Amsterdam. Chelsea, MI:
Bookcrafters.

Hartin, Patrick J. 1991. *James and the 'Q' Sayings of Jesus*. JSNTSup 47.
Sheffield: Sheffield Academic Press.

Kloppenborg, John S. 2004/2009. 'The Reception of the Jesus Tradition in James'. Pages 93–139 in *The Catholic Epistles and the Tradition*. Edited by J. Schlosser. BETL 176. Leuven: Peeters 2004; repr. in *The Catholic Epistles and Apostolic Tradition*, edited by K.-W. Niebuhr and R. T. Wall, 71–100. Waco, TX: Baylor University Press. 2009.

5

Addressees and Purpose

To whom is James addressed? Christians? And if so, Gentile Christians or Jewish Christians? Does the letter imagine the entirety of the Christ movement (irrespective of whether the letter was in fact read by all)? Or does James, whether fictively or actually, envisage a readership of diaspora Jews, some of whom are Christ followers? Finally, what kind of addressees does the letter have in mind? Does James's advocacy for the poor imply that it is addressed mainly to the poor, or to sectors of the population that are in a position to benefit the poor? Are the imagined addressees rural or urban?

Dibelius had been skeptical about the possibility of saying much about James's addressees. This skepticism flowed from his understanding of paraenesis as traditional, unoriginal, unstructured, and eclectic. Given Dibelius's assumptions about James, his conclusions are reasonable. It would be nearly impossible to determine the addressees of a document that merely recycled traditional exhortations without anything original.

Dibelius's estimation of James was wrong. James is not simply recycled bits of traditional wisdom, but exhortations that are based on the Jewish Bible and the Jesus tradition, and which take the form of structures arguments. The new approach to James has also re-opened the possibility of inquiring into the social locations and circumstances that the author imagines for his addressees.

The Distinctive Profile of James

Several features of James are relevant to addressing these questions. First, if as has been argued in Chapter 2, the letter is a pseudepigraphon, it must be realized that not only is the letter not written by James the brother of Jesus in Jerusalem but that the addressees, 'the Twelve tribes in the diaspora', are also fictional. Second, as indicated in Chapter 4, the addressees are expected to recognize as authoritative citations from the Jewish Bible (in Greek); they are expected to regard the upholding of the Law as of central importance; and (at least some of) the audience are expected to recognize the many sayings of Jesus that are embedded in the fabric of James.

Third, as pointed out in Chapter 2, James displays a distinctive lexical profile. The author inclines toward the vocabulary of Hellenistic Judaism, but also uses vocabulary and ideas that were popularized by Stoicism, with its focus on desire (*epithymia*) as a disease of the mind which leads to instability and equivocation in moral judgments. James also draws on some very high-register lexemes that resonate with epic and lyric vocabularies. This lexical and conceptual profile does not, of course, require that the imagined addressees were Stoics or that they routinely read Homer or Euripides. It suggests, however, that the author could expect the addressees to *recognize* these lexical and conceptual registers, much in the same way that a speech today that is peppered with Shakespearean allusions or biblical phrases anticipates audiences that will recognize these allusions, even if the audience would not normally use these words and phrases as a part of their regular working vocabularies. In other words, we should imagine for James an audience that is at least moderately educated.

Fourth is the list of items missing from James. There are no references to the management of households, as there are in Colossians, Ephesians, 1 Peter, and the Pastoral letters. Rahab is cited as an example of one who has righteous deeds, but women are otherwise mentioned only at 2:15 ('if a brother or a sister are naked ....'). James is silent about families, parents, children, and slaves, the usual topics of the household codes in NT letters. He uses *anthrōpos* in a way that might be gender-inclusive at 1:7, 19; 2:20, 24; and 3:8, 9; but he also uses *anēr* ('male') in generalizing formulations such as 'the double-minded man is unstable in all his ways' (1:8), 'blessed is the man who endures testing' (1:12), and 'if someone does not stumble in what he says this is a perfect man' (3:2). It is a rich man who enters the assembly in Jas 2:2. The author refers to the prohibition of adultery (Jas 2:11). But he does not mention prohibition of re-marriage after divorce, where the Synoptic gospels treat remarriage after divorce as constituting an injury to the first wife (Mt 5:32; Lk

16:18). James's vocative 'adulteresses' in 4:4 is not evidence of women in the group, but rather a matter of gender-shaming—addressing men as women (cf. Ezek 23:45). The author thus seems to think in androcentric categories. Hence, the repeated address, *adelphoi* (*mou agapētoi*) should probably be rendered '(my beloved) brothers' rather than 'brothers and sisters', with the NRSV.

Fifth and perhaps most puzzlingly, James fails to mention specifically Christian beliefs and practices where one might otherwise expect him to do so. There are no references to the death or resurrection of Christ, even in connection with the mentions of the enduring of testing. Compare 1 Pet 1:6–7; 4:12–13, where testing is immediately linked to Christ's suffering. Forgiveness of sins in Jas 5:20 is not connected with Christ's actions. Although James anticipates the Parousia in Jas 5:7–8, there is no elaboration of Christ's role at the Parousia, as there is in 1 Thess 4:13–17 and 1 Corinthians 15. Nor are there references to baptism or the Lord's Supper. As McNeile once observed, none of what might be taken as distinctively Christian requires that it be so understood: 'my brothers' is not exclusively an address of members of the Jesus movement but appears as a regular address to Jews living in the diaspora (2 Macc. 1:1; 2 Bar. 78.2; 79.1; 80.1; 82.1; *b.Sanh.* 11b; Elephantine letters B13). *Ho kyrios* ('the Lord') refers to God unambiguously at 3:9 and 5:4, and probably at 1:7, 4:10, 15, and 5:10. The references in Jas 5:7, 8, 11, 14, 15 are ambiguous and could refer to either God or Christ. There are only two unambiguous references to Christ as *kyrios* at 1:1 and 2:1, the latter raising suspicions that it is an interpolation. The phrases 'birth by a word of truth' (1:18), 'the law of perfect freedom' (1:25), and 'the royal law' (2:8) are probable reference to the Torah rather than some distinctively Christian message. 'The noble name' (2:7) might refer either to the name of God or that of Christ; 'assembly' (*ekklēsia*) *in* 5:14 could be interpreted either in reference to synagogues or to Christian assemblies; and the *parousia* of the Lord (5:7, 8) and the 'judge who is standing at the door' (5:9) could refer to the Lord coming in judgment or to a belief in the Parousia of Christ (McNeile 1923, 88–95).

Finally, the examples of loyalty, endurance, and prayer are drawn from the Jewish Bible—Abraham, Rahab, Job, Elijah—rather than from Christian narratives. Yet there is no mention of Israel, Moses, Jerusalem, the Temple, priests, Sabbath, Passover, circumcision, or the avoidance of unclean foods. James never uses the term *ta ethnē* to refer to non-Jews and the mention of 'the world' in 1:27 and

4:4 has nothing to do with a mission to non-Jews. On the other hand, the Law (*nomos*) is mentioned throughout (1:25; 2:8–12; 4:11), where James speaks of investigating, persevering, keeping, and acting in accordance with the Law as positive values. The Law supplies the norms of judgment (2:12).

The Addressees of James

Any reconstruction of the intended audience of James must take into account both what James says and the issues about which he is silent.

The Twelve Tribes That Are in the Diaspora

The letter is addressed to the 'twelve tribes that are in the diaspora'. As pointed out above, this address seems impossible: the twelve tribes had not existed since the eighth century BCE. Nevertheless, the belief persisted that the twelve tribes continued to exist and would be restored in the future, encouraged perhaps by 2 Chron 10:17 and 11:13–17 which suggested that some from the Northern tribes settled in the South during the division of Israel into the Northern and Southern Kingdoms. Or these hopes may have been inspired by Isa 11:11–12, Isa 49:9, Jer 23:7–8, and Ezek 37:19–22, which speak of the restoration of Israel. Or again the expectation of restoration may have come about through the belief that the Northern tribes had somehow survived and were now located across the Euphrates (4 Ezra 13:39–47). As Sanders points out, the idea of an eschatological restoration of Israel to its original integrity was widespread (1992, 289–94). For example, the diaspora letter in 2 Baruch 78–87, written in the late first century or early second CE, has Baruch writing to the nine and one-half tribes located across the river Euphrates (78:1) and promising that God 'will gather together again those who were dispersed' (78:7). Texts from Qumran evidence hopes about the restoration of the twelve tribes (1QM III 13; V 1; CDC X 5; 11QTemple XXIV 10). The same hopes are witnessed in several early texts from the early Christ movement (Q 22:28–30 [Mt 19:28 ∥ Lk 22:30]; Acts 26:7; Rev 21:12).

The most obvious way to read Jas 1:1, then, is that it engages the belief in the continued existence of the twelve tribes, now located somewhere in the diaspora. It is no coincidence that the putative author is James (i.e., Jacob), the namesake of the patriarch Jacob whose twelve sons were the eponymous ancestors of those twelve tribes. A letter to the twelve tribes could well be an originally Jewish document, lightly Christianized, and analogous to the Testament of the Twelve patriarchs.

As noted in Chapter 2, this view depends on the supposition that 'the Lord Jesus Christ' in 1:1 and 2:1 are interpolations. The syntax of 2:1 is overloaded and there are good reasons to think that the text might be corrupt (Mayor 1892, cxciii; Allison 2013a, 382–3; Kloppenborg 2007). There is little reason, however, to treat the name of Jesus in 1:1 as an addition any more than there was reason to follow Harnack or Llewelyn in considering the whole of 1:1 as an addition that converted a collection of sayings or an essay into a letter (see above, Chapter 3). Hence, on the literal reading of 'twelve tribes', James is a letter from a distinguished member of the Jesus movement to Jews in the diaspora.

The phrase 'twelve tribes' is only part of the puzzle. 'Diaspora' is the other part. It is now common to suppose that 'diaspora' refers to Christ followers, both Jewish and non-Jewish, residing outside of Palestine. In this case, 'diaspora' cannot refer literally to an ethnic diaspora, since there is no reason to think that all the Christ followers in Macedonia, Achaia, Asia, or Italy were all diasporic, still less from a single ethnic diaspora. The term must be used metaphorically, of Christ followers scattered throughout the Mediterranean. Dibelius puts the case this way:

If the author [of James] were a Jew, then without further ado we would take this expression in the strict sense of Jews outside Palestine. But since the author and his readers are Christians, difficulties arise .... [I]f the readers are Christians then the designation 'twelve tribes in the Diaspora' must express just this Christian character. So then, we are forced to a metaphorical interpretation, and there is only one which is possible: namely, to consider the designation as a reference to the true Israel, for whom heaven is home and earth is only a foreign country, i.e., a Diaspora .... But in this case, it seems to me that there is no indication that the addresses are of Jewish extraction, since the entire expression must be construed in a completely metaphorical sense.

(Dibelius 1921/1976, 66)

1 Peter attests the metaphorical use of 'diaspora'. 1 Pet 1:1 addresses the 'elect resident aliens of the diaspora of Pontus, Galatia, Cappadocia, Asia, and Bithynia'. This cannot represent a single ethnic diaspora. Of course there might be diasporic Jews among the addressees of 1 Peter, but 1 Pet 1:14 and 4:3–4 also indicate that the addressees included non-Jews. Hence, we are obliged to see 1 Peter as an instance of 'diaspora' used metaphorically and applied to Christ followers in these regions of Asia. Philo (*Praem.* 115–16) also used 'diaspora' in a metaphorical sense, to connote the soul alienated from virtue and wisdom by evil. This 'diasporic' soul then anticipates a 'restoration to the land of virtue and wisdom and (a return) from a spiritual diaspora (*ek diasporas psychikēs*)' (cf. also *Conf.* 197). In the second century CE Justin Martyr also used 'diaspora' metaphorically when he interpreted the story of Joshua's conquest typologically: like Joshua, Christ led the people into the holy land and thereby overcame the 'diaspora of the people' by distributing spiritual goods (*Dial.* 113.3).

If 'diaspora' in Jas 1:1 refers to Christ followers throughout the Mediterranean, there is another consequence: Jas 1:1 would be the first instance in Christian literature of the term 'twelve tribes' being transferred to the Christian group as a whole. In fact, it becomes the *sole* instance of 'twelve tribes' being applied to Christ followers. Elsewhere the designation 'the twelve tribes' refers only to collective Israel and is *never* elsewhere attested as a sobriquet for Christ followers as an entity distinct from Israel. This is true of the three texts mentioned above, Q 22:28–30, Acts 26:7, and Rev 21:12. It is also true of 1 Clem. 55.6 (in a variant reading, in which the adjective 'twelve-tribe' [*dōdekaphylon*] is interpolated into the phrase 'the nation of Israel') and in the *Protoevangelium of James* (2.3–4).

It is of course possible that Jas 1:1 is the sole text to use 'twelve tribes' to refer to Christ groups. But in the absence of other signals in the incipit of James or elsewhere in the letter that would oblige the interpreter to suspect a metaphorical usage, the phrase 'the twelve tribes in the diaspora' ought to be taken in its ordinary geographical sense. James Mayor quipped:

I cannot think … that the bare phrase *tais dōdeka phylais tais en tē diaspora* is susceptible of a … figurative meaning, any more than the phrase used by the Pharisees in John vii.35, 'Will he go '*eis tēn diasporan tōn Hellēnōn* [to the diaspora of the Greeks].

(Mayor 1892, 31)

'The twelve tribes that are in the diaspora', hence, is not a metaphor for Christ followers who are away from their real home, nor is 'the twelve tribes' an otherwise unattested designation for Christ followers. This leaves us with several conundrums. The author on the one hand makes no attempt to disguise that he is a Christ follower and yet appears to be addressing diaspora Jews. There are no explicit references to the distinctives of the Christ movement, yet the letter is peppered with allusions to Jesus's sayings and seems to take aim at Paul or at least a Pauline distinction between loyalty/faith and deeds. It has the marks of a learned composition and it has an urban audience in mind, probably in Alexandria or possibly Rome, both of which had large diasporic Jewish populations that had emigrated from Palestine or had been taken to Rome as slaves or prisoners.

Reviving a suggestion of A. H. McNeile that James wrote to both Jews and Christians to encourage the 'highest standard of ethics for Jew and for Christian' (1923, 95), Allison proposed that James reflects a sector of the Jesus movement that sought to keep its relations with other Jews eirenic. James's purpose was not to proselytize but 'to promote tolerance, to gain sympathy for Christians in a context where there is perhaps growing antipathy' (Allison 2001, 568). Hence, Allison understands the address of James to refer to diasporic Jews (some of whom might be Christ followers).

Allison suggests 4QMMT as an analogy. This document, although it was composed in the sectarian community of Qumran, is apparently addressed to those outside the community. It is largely silent about the distinctive features and beliefs of the Qumran group, such as their belief in two messiahs, and the special role that they assigned to the Teacher of Righteousness. Instead, 4QMMT appeals to general principles that would be persuasive to those outside the Qumran group (see Collins 1997, 81). Its suppression of the sectarian aspects of the *yaḥad* is in the interests of achieving peaceful relations with others.

Three groups are on 4QMMT's discursive horizon: the 'we/us' who elaborate on various rules that pertain to sacrifice and other matters; and the addresses ('you') who are assumed to be in general agreement with 'us' about those rules and to whom the 'we' appeal for understanding. The closing summary illustrates the group's appeal for understanding:

We have written to you some of the works of the Torah which we think are good for you and for your people, for we saw that you have intellect and knowledge of the Law. Reflect on all these matters and seek from him so that he may support your counsel and keep far from you the evil scheming{s} and the counsel of Belial so that at the end of time you may rejoice in finding that some of our words are true. And it shall be reckoned to you as justice when you do what is upright and good before him, for your good and that of Israel.

(4QMMT 112–118; García Martínez and
Tigchelaar 1997, 803)

In addition to the 'we' and the 'you', 4QMMT identifies a third group ('they') which is contrasted with the 'we': for example, 'concerning the thank offering which *they* postpone from one day to another, *we think* that it should be eaten ... on the day of their sacrifice' (4QMMT 14).

4QMMT expects that 'you' will be sympathetic to the recommendations of the 'we' group and distance themselves from the 'they'. Later documents from Qumran suggest that 4QMMT was not successful in its eirenic intentions. The pesher on the Psalms, 4QpPs[a] on Ps 37:32–33, seems to refer to 4QMMT when it speaks of the 'Law and the Torah' that the Teacher of Righteousness sent to the 'Wicked Priest' (as he was called by the time 4QpPs[a] was composed). It so, 4QMMT had been sent to priestly authorities in Jerusalem in order to cultivate understanding. But the effort failed. It is possible even that 4QMMT was never sent to anyone outside the *yaḥad* and was only used internally. That would make some sense of the several copies of 4QMMT that were found in Cave 4. In that case the 'you' and the 'they' are fictive constructions. Whichever is the case, it remains that the letter refrains from referring to practices and beliefs that would distinguish 'us' from 'you' and addresses the 'you' as if they could be appealed to on the basis of common values.

Is James like 4QMMT? The groups in James can also be parsed into 'us', 'you', and 'they'. James (i.e., James's Christ followers) addresses diasporic Jews with the affectionate title 'my beloved brothers'. These addressees are assumed to regard Abraham as their father (2:21) and understand the examples of Rahab (2:25), Job and the prophets (5:10–11), and Elijah (5:17). They also claim to 'fulfil' to the 'royal law' (2:8). James's address to the 'you' can also be more aggressive: he is prepared to admonish potential misdeeds, calling those who cultivate friendship with the world 'adulteresses'

(4:4) accusing them of being double-minded (4:8). Yet at the end of 3:13–4:10 James sounds a more eirenic note, assuring the addressees that submission to God will lead to them being exalted (4:10).

For the author, the 'they' are less clearly defined. They include the rich who abuse the addressees (2:6b-7) and probably those who are apostrophized in 4:13–5:6 (the arrogant, the rich, and predatory landowners). They might also include the 'blockhead' in 2:20, who emphasizes faith to the exclusion of deeds. It seems unlikely that the latter would have read the letter, any more than 4QMMT's 'they' were imagined as real interlocutors.

If we follow McNeile and Allison, the puzzling contents of the letter become intelligible: 'James', who makes no pretense about his connection with the Jesus movement, nevertheless composed a letter that has in mind diaspora Jews as potential readers. The distinctives of the Jesus movement are suppressed, although a reader familiar with the sayings of Jesus would have no difficulty in seeing the allusions to those sayings, scattered throughout the letter. The explicit arguments of James are based on appeals to the Jewish Bible, in particular the Decalogue, Leviticus 19, well-known texts from the prophets, and the *exempla* of Abraham, Rahab, the prophets, Job, and Elijah. In other words, James is framed as a discourse to Jews and offers arguments designed to appeal to Jews based on common values. But at another level it speaks to Christ followers.

There are analogies to this kind of bi-focal discourse—that is, discourse that operates at an ostensible level and another level that is meant for insiders. In the wake of the terrorist attack of 9/11, President George W. Bush delivered two public speeches to the American people, one on September 11, before the terrorists had been identified, and a second on October 7 announcing attacks on Al-Qaeda camp in Afghanistan. The October 7 speech, as Bruce Lincoln points out, had little explicit to say about religion. It did not even mention God except in the final formula, 'May God continue to bless America,' which was an adaptation of the more typical formula, 'May God bless America.' This reserve in relation to explicit religious speech is in keeping with the idea of America as a state in which religion and the state are separate. Yet as Lincoln points out, the speech was riddled with allusions to the Bible. For example, its description of the terrorists 'burrow[ing] deeper into caves' recalls the description of the impious of Rev 6:15, who 'hid in the caves and among the rocks of the mountains' trying to evade judgment. Bush's description of the terrorists and their collaborators as 'killers of innocents' recalls Exod 23:7 and Matthew's story of the slaughter of the innocent in Matthew 2.

This 'double coding', as Lincoln calls it, was designed to appeal to both the American public in general, who expect their president to speak as the leader of a secular state, *and* the portion of that public that understands America as a nation of religious commitments, 'One nation under God'. For the latter:

> This conversion of secular political speech into religious discourse invests otherwise merely human events with transcendent significance. By the end, America's adversaries have been redefined as enemies of God, and current events have been constituted as confirmation of Scripture.
>
> (Lincoln 2006, 32)

James, too, has two audiences in mind. On the one hand, James appeals to Jews, whose sensibilities are addressed in James's appeals to 'the perfect law of freedom' (1:25) and the characterization of the law as the final arbiter of behaviour (2:8, 9, 10, 11; 4:11–12). They are meant to conclude that the leader of the Jesus movement is not opposed to the Torah, a charge that was leveled at Paul by sectors of Christ followers represented by the *Letter of Peter to James* (2.2–3). As Allison point out, James addresses diaspora Jews without explicit allusion to distinctively Christian principles, since these would hardly have been persuasive to diasporic Jews (Allison 2013b). On the other hand, it also appeals to Christ followers to maintain a way of life that is informed by the psychagogy of Hellenistic Judaism, illustrating via sayings of Jesus that they are meant to recognize the alignment between Jesus's sayings and the ideal way of life for diaspora Jews.

Urban and Middling Addressees

What sort of addressees does the letter imagine? There has been much recent inquiry into the social level of the early Jesus movement, in particular those located in the cities of the empire. Were they uniformly among the poorest, living just as the subsistence level? Or did they include persons of higher social and economic standing?

The consensus toward the end of the twentieth century, for which Wayne Meeks's *The First Urban Christians* (1983) was largely responsible, was that urban Christ groups in the first century lacked both the very bottom and the very top of urban society. Neither the ultra-rich (senators, equestrians, decurions) nor the extremely poor were present. The Jesus movement flourished in the numerically significant 'middling' group, consisting of artisans, domestic slaves, freedmen and freedwomen (i.e., former slaves), and a few with more modest levels of wealth who might serve as benefactors of Christ groups. That consensus has not changed much in the past forty years (Kloppenborg 2019).

There are indications that the second century saw some changes. A careful analysis of Hermas suggests that the Roman groups he addressed included some persons of wealth—probable well-off freedmen—who were in a financial position to spend large sums to purchase fields and houses (Sim. 1.1.1–8). Later in that century Tertullian claims that Christ groups included some equestrians and perhaps even senators (Tertullian, *Apol.* 37.4). During the second century, at least some Christ groups were on an upward trajectory in terms of the members they could expect to recruit.

What of the addressees of James? In the first place, it is clear that James's audience is urban, not rural. There are, of course, rural images, as there are in practically all ancient literature. James evokes the images of harvesting (5:4), of farmers awaiting their crops (5:7) and, as already observed in Chapter 2, the early and late rains and the *ḥamṣin* wind, all images that make sense to agriculturalists. Alicia Batten noticed James is also replete with urban images: the *synagōgē* (2:2, i.e., a building), law courts (2:6), traveling merchants (4:13), and absentee landlords who live in luxury (5:1–5) (Batten 2014, 84, 88). Even more significant is the observation made in Chapter 4 that in paraphrasing Q 12:33–34, which reflects rural Palestine, Jas 5:2–3 has 'urbanized' the saying.

There are several other examples of urbanization of the sayings of Jesus. Jas 1:12 adapts the 'persecution beatitude' (Q 6:22–23), which in its rural environment relied on the metaphor of agricultural workers receiving wages:

Blessed are you when they insult and persecute you and say every kind of evil against you because of the Son of Man. Be glad and exult, for your wages (*misthos*) in heaven are great. For this is how they persecuted the prophets before you.

The normal Greek term for agricultural day-laborers was *ergatai* (Q 10:2) and their wages were *misthoi*. James uses both *ergatai* and *misthoi* in Jas 5:4 where he speaks of agricultural laborers being defrauded by landowners. But it is important to know that landlords were often absentees, residing in towns and cities and living off the income from their properties. James is critical of these city-folk, because they 'live luxuriously from land and self-indulgently'.

When one compares Q's version of the persecution beatitude (Q 6:23) to what James has in 1:12 the shift from countryside to city becomes obvious:

> Blessed is the man who endures testing, for being approved (*dokimos*), he will receive the crown (*stephanos*) of life, which he promised to those who love him.
>
> (1:12)

While Q speaks of those who endure persecution receiving *wages*, James speaks not of persecution but testing. The recompense is a *stephanos*, a crown. Crowns of gold or olive leaves were the typical means of recognizing meritorious achievement in civic contexts. James's term *dokimos* (approved) is also a term that belongs to urban vocabularies, reflecting the practice of vetting (*dokimazō*) candidates for citizenship or for public office. That is, James has shifted the register of the saying from the countryside to the city, from agricultural wages to civic honours.

A propos of James's paraphrase of Q's saying on not being a slave (*douleuein*) to both God and Mammon (Q 16:13), Alicia Batten (2014) notes significant changes in Jas 4:4:

> Don't you know that friendship with the world is enmity to God; whoever then wants to be a friend of the world becomes an enemy of God.

James avoids Q's condemnation of money (Mammon), since as Batten notes, money was unavoidable in an urban context. Q's metaphor of slavery (*douleuein*) is also replaced by the notion of contrasting friendships, with God and with the world. It is not that slavery was absent from cities or that the notion of friendship was foreign to rural environments. In popular philosophical discourse, however, the wise person was supposed to be a friend of God, since she or he participated in the knowledge of God. Philo refers to Moses as a friend of God (*Cher.* 1.49; *Moses* 1:156) and the *Testament of Abraham* calls Abraham God's friend (*T. Abr.* 1.7; 4.7). Note also that Jas 2:23 calls Abraham God's friend, adding this to his quotation of Gen 15:7. James's reformulation of Q 16:13 produced a saying that recast Q's contrast in a form that was more amenable to a semi-educated, urban audience, which thought not in terms of slavery to God but friendship with the divine.

I have already noted in Chapter 4 that Jas 5:2–3 transformed Q 12:33–34, a saying that conceived wealth in typically agricultural terms: woolen clothing that can be damaged by moths, food that insects destroy, and other goods that house-breakers can steal. James, however, measures wealth in clothing that can be moth-eaten and *jewelry* (silver and gold) that can tarnish and corrode. Recall also that this is how he described the imaginary rich man who entered the assembly: a gold-fingered man (i.e., with prominent rings), wearing brilliant (*lampra*) clothing (2:2). This is a characteristically urban image: grandees in all their finery, expecting to get the best seats at the dinner, and adulation from their clients. It is telling that James imagines this as a possibility in his day, an indication that he is already aware of the upward social trajectory of Christ groups that is attested elsewhere by second-century Christian sources.

What about the social level of those addressees? Dibelius stressed the presence in James's discourse of the 'piety of the poor', a theological construct which first aligned piety with poverty as a rhetorical device by which to criticize wealth and power, but which eventually came to *equate* being poor with being pious (1921/1976, 39–45). Dibelius concluded that the latter was the case for James:

Ja(me)s can express his sympathy with the poor with so little reserve because for him being poor and being Christian were coincidental concepts.

(Dibelius 1921/1976, 44)

For Dibelius, there the wealthy were not part of his group. James

shouted threats out the window for all the world to hear, no doubt he still did not have in his own house very many of these rich who are attacked.

(Dibelius 1921/1976, 45)

Dibelius's view is based on such texts as Jas 2:5 ('has not chosen the poor of the world to be rich in faith and to be heirs of the kingdom?') and the attack on the wealthy in Jas 4:13–5:6. Indeed, Maynard-Reid (1987) concluded that the groups addressed by James had no wealthy members and regarded the rich only as oppressors.

Yet it should be kept in mind that 'rich' and 'poor' are extremely slippery terms and have very little relationship to income. 'Rich' and 'poor' are always comparative terms, used by those to refer to others who are better or worse off than them. Commenting on the scene in Jas 2:2–3, Roland Deines observes:

> What is obvious is that James regards his addressees as neither belonging to the societal stratum of the rich one nor to that of the poor in his ragged clothes.
>
> (Deines 2014, 347)

Were the Jacobean groups only the indigent, at the bottom on Mediterranean society, there would be no likelihood of a visit from a 'gold-fingered' man. Favoritism and deference to the rich becomes an issue in Jas 2:1–13 because the possibility of such visits is now a real one. James positions his addressees somewhere in the middle, faced both with the possibility of having to decide how to respond to the approach of, for example, a wealthy freedman who might expect deference on the one hand, and how to deal with the very poor who might come seeking aid from the group. On balance, James is more hostile to wealth and the wealthy than sympathetic, but like Hermas he must consider how to respond to the threats to group integrity that the very wealthy represented.

Rebecca Sanfridson has recently argued that in Jas 2:2 the author assumes that he is addressing Jews who have a synagogue—that is, owned a building. This would have required funds to maintain the building and have meals. If, as seems likely, that Jas 2:1–13 aims at limiting or discouraging patronage by super-wealthy outsiders (see also Kloppenborg 1999), then, Sanfridson reasons, James must also have known his addressees 'to be wealthy enough to economically support their group life solely with membership fees and internal collections/donations'. She suggests that this implies members of 'relatively high socio-economic status' (Sanfridson 2018, 26).

A lot depends on what we might mean by 'relatively high socio-economic status'. It is true that *synagōgē* in Jas 2:2 means a building (which has better and worse places to sit or stand). Synagogue buildings were sometimes built collectively by community members, which of course presupposes that many members of the group had sufficient income to underwrite a construction project (e.g., GRA III 154, 156–158, 186). Not all synagogues were built by the group, however. The Theodotus inscription (CIIP I/1 9; Jerusalem, first century CE) and the Julia Severa inscription (*MAMA* VI 264, Akmonia, Phrygia, late first century CE) indicate that in some cases, wealthy donors built synagogues for client groups of Jews. Yet even if in these cases, such synagogues would still have required upkeep and support for their ongoing activities. Hence, we can agree with Sanfridson that at least some of those addressed by James must have been persons of some means, able to support a synagogue. Thus, while James is critical of wealth and the improper attachment to wealth, he also plainly supposes that his addressees supported their respective groups, and were in a position to aid for the poor. This takes money and resources.

James and Psychagogy

I have argued in Chapter 3 that James is an example of paraenesis or moral exhortation in letter form. What sets James off from some other forms of paraenetic discourse, which tended to be sententious, is the construction of extended argumentative units of a dozen verses or so forming a coherent argument. This inclines James toward one particular form of moral exhortation, protreptic.

A distinctive feature of James, and one related to its argumentative form, is that James is not simply a list of do's and don'ts akin to what is found, for example, in Ps-Isocrates's *To Demonicus*, *Ps-Phocylides*, or the *Sentences of Sextus*. James is keenly interested in the conditions of the soul from which moral actions flow. The distinction between sententious paraenesis and what I believe that James is pursuing is the subject of Seneca's *Epistulae* 94–95. In *Epistula* 94 Seneca had argued that individual precepts were indeed useful for guiding conduct. But attending to the conditions of the soul was a necessary part of moral instruction and this required not individual precepts but more complex arguments:

> It will therefore be of no avail to give precepts unless you first remove the conditions that are likely to stand in the way of precepts; it will do no more good than to place weapons by your side and bring yourself near the foe without having your hands free to use those weapons. The soul, in order to deal with the precepts which we offer, must first be set free.
>
> (Seneca, *Epistulae morales* 95.37)

Although James still resorts to some individual precepts, especially at the end of the letter (5:7–20), the majority of the letter takes the form of structured argumentative units. These units focus on the factors which, in Seneca's words, stand in the way of precepts, that is, those factors that obstruct one's relationship with God and inhibit truly moral action. The search for wisdom is important, but a soul that is clouded by desire cannot truly pursue wisdom. Teaching is important; but the teacher must first be able to control his tongue. The cultivation of the soul is for James the prerequisite for moral action.

Of course, James does not offer the kind of detailed philosophical paraenesis found in Seneca's letters. Instead, his psychagogy takes the form of paraphrases of sayings of Jesus and allusions to the Jewish Bible. Chapter 4 discussed the way James treated both citations from the Jewish Bible and sayings of Jesus, employing the technique of *aemulatio* or rhetorical paraphrase. In several instances James introduced into these sayings the principles of Stoic psychagogy, for example the idea that desire and passions were pathologies that infect and unbalance the soul, impeding its ability to benefit from God's wisdom.

Emotions and the Training of the Self

Let us revisit James's *aemulatio* of Q 11:9–10 (Mt 7:7–8 ‖ Lk 11:9–10), discussed in Chapter 4. The Q saying is tripartite ('ask and it will be given, seek and you will find, knock and it will be opened'). James only took over the first pair of verbs from Q. It was observed that in Q the objects of petition were matters of subsistence: bread, fish, debt cancellation, and freedom from testing (Q 11:3–4, 11–13); for James the object of prayer is *sophia*, wisdom. In place of Q's extraordinary claim that 'everyone who asks receives', James substitutes a characterization of God: God gives to all single-mindedly (*haplōs*) and without reproach (1:5). To state that God acts singly (i.e., without equivocation or hesitation) and without reproach is to provide a subtle counterpoint to James's attack on being 'double-minded' (*dipsychos*). James's portrait of God is also a counterpoint to the scenario of deference to a wealthy patron described in 2:2–4. Patronage institutionalized status differences and at least in the view of moralists like Juvenal (*Sat.* 1.127–128; 3.122–24) and Martial (*Epigrams* 12.26.13–14; 9.100), led to the humiliation of clients (see Kloppenborg 1999). For James, however, God gives *without* reproach (1:5).

The introduction of a characterization of God as *haplos* is an example of what rhetoricians called *insinuatio* or a 'subtle approach', used in the exordium when the orator anticipated resistance to his argument. James's audience would likely have no difficulty in embracing the characterization of God who gives generously or single-mindedly (*haplōs*). This characterization, however, swiftly becomes the counterpoint to James's real interest, the description of the conditions of the soul that make the reception of wisdom impossible: being double-minded. James calls for nothing less than a transformation of the self:

> But let him ask in trust, disputing nothing, for whoever disputes is like the surf of the sea, blown and tossed by the wind; [7] for let not such a person suppose that he will receive anything from the Lord, [8] a double-minded man (*dipsychos*), unstable (*akatastatos*) in all his ways.
>
> (James 1:6–8)

The conditions of the double-minded man are then elaborated: he disputes or wavers (*diakrinomai*) and is thus like the sea, fundamentally unstable. James traces this instability to the inability to understand or endure testing (1:12). The root of this inability is desire (*epithymia*), which drags (*exeklō*) and lures (*deleazō*) the soul, eventually infecting it with sin (1:14–15). The wavering man makes the mistake of thinking that God is the source of his testing (1:13, 17); but the reality is that the source of testing is his own desire (1:13). Thus, for James, there is a cognitive defect in the soul, caused by the inability to understand the pathological nature of desire, and it is this that leads to sin.

When James returns to Q 10:9–10 in Jas 4:2b-3, he first restates Jas 1:5 in the negative, and then qualifies it:

You do not have because you don't ask. You ask and do not receive, because you ask wrongly, in order to expend it on your pleasures.

This elaborates the argument of Jas 1:5–14 that God should be petitioned for wisdom and in a way that is not infected by desire or the craving for pleasure. Acting out of these desires makes it impossible to receive wisdom. This in turn explains the catalogue of evils that James elaborates in 3:13–4:2: rivalry, factionalism, instability, foul deeds, wars, battles, envy, and jealousy.

I have already touched briefly on another aspect of James's psychagogy. In connection with his instruction on the control of the tongue (Jas 3:1–12), James paraphrases Gen 1:26b. But instead of using the LXX's *archō* ('to rule') in relation to humankind's relation to the animal world, James prefers *damazō*. This is because the verb alludes to Odysseus' 'training' of the self through suffering and hardship. As I have explained, by the early Roman period, the verb (and the image of Odysseus) had become a metaphor for self-mastery, especially of the emotions. Philo had used the verb as a metaphor for the control of pleasure (*hēdonē*) (*Spec.* 2.104–106) and Plutarch applied to verb to the control of the passions (*pathē*) (Plutarch, *De virtute morali* 451D). The verb was thus entirely appropriate in James's discourse on the control of tongue.

James displays many affinities with the moralizing literature of Hellenistic Judaism, in particular some of the tractates of the *Testaments of the Twelve Patriarchs*. For example, the *Testament of Asher* has as its focus the 'two faces of evil and virtue'. The author argues in a manner like Jas 2:8–11, that for the person who observes one commandment but violates another, 'the whole is evil'. This is a version of the Stoic principle, *qui unum autem habet vitium, omnia habet*, 'whoever has one vice has them all' (Seneca, *De beneficiis* 5.15.1). James states it thus: 'Whoever keeps the whole law, but stumbles in one feature, has become liable to all' (Jas 2:10). The point is that the moral law is unitary, so that the violation of one provision amounts to a violation of all. To claim to observe the Golden Rule, or as James calls it, the Royal Law (Lev 19:18), but at the same time to display favouritism vitiates the claim to be faithful to the Law. Lev 19:15 is inseparable from Lev 19:18.

The *Testament of Benjamin*, whose theme is the 'purification of the mind', also offers striking parallel to the contents of James. The *Testament of Benjamin* expressly contrasts 'singleness' as a mode of cognition with doubleness and its pathological consequences. So close to James's topics of interest is *T.Benj.* 6.1–7 that could even be regarded as a précis of James:

[1] The disposition of the good man is not in the control of the deception of the spirit of Beliar, for the angel of peace guides his soul. [2] He does not look with passion at corruptible things, nor gathers wealth out of a desire of	James
pleasure (*philēdonia*). [3] He does not delight in pleasure	1:10
(*hēdonē*); he does not cause his neighbour grief; he does	4:3
not fill himself with luxuries (*tryphē*), he is not deceived by	4:12; 5:5
the lifting up (*meteōrismoi*) of eyes (i.e., favouritism): the	2:1, 9
Lord is his portion. [4] The good disposition does not receive glory or dishonour from people, and it does not know any	
deceit or lies (*pseudos*) or fighting (*machē*), or reviling; for	3:14; 4:1
the Lord dwells in him (*en autō katoikei*) and illumines his	4:5
soul, and he rejoices toward all people always. [5] The good	3:10
mind does not have two tongues, of blessing and cursing (*eulogia kai katarē*), of hybris and honour, of grief and joy, of quietness and disturbance (*tarachē*), of hypocrisy	
and of truth, of poverty and of wealth; but it has a single	1:27; 4:8
disposition, uncorrupt and pure (*kathara*), concerning all	1:8; 4:8
people. [6] It does not have double sight nor double hearing,	2:12
for in everything which it does, or speaks, or sees, it knows that the Lord watches over the soul. [7] And he cleanses	
(*kathairo*) his mind that he may not be condemned by	1:27; 4:8
people or by God. And (by contrast) every work of Beliar is	2:9; 5:9
twofold and possesses no singleness (*haplotēs*).	1:5

Both James and the *Testament of Benjamin* mythologize the soul, caught between the devil (James) or Beliar (*T.Benj.*). As the extract above indicates, there are strong lexical and thematic overlap between James and *T.Benj.* 6: the divided self is a source of vice and of such contradictory behaviours as blessing and cursing; God indwells the soul, or at least the souls of those who have pure minds; desire and pleasure are threats to the self; there must be consistency between speech and action; and luxurious living is a threat to the soul.

James's dramatic description of the soul, dragged and lured by desire also finds parallels in Philo:

> For there is nothing which, lured by pleasure (*pros hēdonēs deleasthen*), is not dragged (*eilkystai*) and caught by her thickly-twisted nets, from which escape is very difficult.
>
> (*Agr.* 103–5)

> For if the soul is driven by desire (*epithymia*) or lured by pleasure (*hyph' hēdonēs deleazetai*) or diverted from its course by fear or shrunken by grief or helpless in the grip of anger, it makes itself a slave, and indeed one who has many owners. But if it vanquishes ignorance by prudence, incontinence by moderation, cowardice by courage, and greed by righteousness, it gains not only freedom from slavery but the gift of ruling as well.
>
> (*Prob.* 159; also *Her.* 269)

I am not suggesting here that James is dependent upon the *Testament of Benjamin* or upon Philo. The convergences are not sufficient to make a credible case for borrowing or influence. These convergences, however, suggest that Stoic psychology has had an impact on each of these sources.

The philosophical pedigrees of James and the *Testaments* are indistinct, because neither explicitly discusses the philosophical questions posed by Greek thinkers on origin, nature, and control of the passions. Nevertheless, a key feature of Stoicism that is shared by Philo, the *Testaments*, and James is the notion that the passions, including desire (*epithymia*) and pleasure (*hēdonē*), are based on faulty judgments concerning the Good and, if embraced, disturb the soul. It is not a matter of two warring principles within the soul; it is instead the inability of the soul to grasp and hold onto a vision of God and of the Good, and this in turn results shifting back and forth between opinions, a phenomenon that Stoics called 'instability' (*akatastasia*, Diogenes Laertius 7.110) or 'vacillation' (Seneca, *Ep.* 52.1; cf. *De tranquillitate animi* 2.7), or 'fluttering' (Arius Didymus, SVF 3.663). This is the essence of being 'double-minded': being unable to decide and hence, to act. Thus, for both James and the *Testament of Benjamin* the imperfect man can bless and curse at the same time, and according to James can uphold Lev 19:18 but at the same time violate Lev 19:15. The perfect man cannot.

Curiously, while the Stoic diagnosis of passions was that they were dangerous, Stoics also identified 'good emotions' (*eupatheia*), especially 'joy' (*chara*), which they distinguished from pleasure (Seneca *Ep.* 59). Pleasures are transient, but joy flows from a grasp of the truth. Just as Stoics held that the vices were unitary, so they also held that all true virtues and goods of the soul were equal and equivalent: joy, endurance, tranquility, simplicity, generosity, constancy, and equanimity (Seneca, *Ep.* 66.12–13). Hence, if one reads James through the Stoic notion of virtue, it is not surprising that he begins by speaking of the endurance of testing and joy in the same breath (1:2–4) while immediately eschewing desire as pathological.

Perfection through Endurance

Since James does not offer theoretical reflections on the soul and its constitution, it is impossible to know how his thoughts align with other elements of Stoicism or with Philo's hybridization of Stoicism and Platonism. James, however, did seem to embrace the Stoic notion that perfection was possible. At 3:2 James ventures:

> For all of us stumble. If someone does not stumble in what he says, this is a perfect man, able to bridle even the entire body.
> (3:2)

This might appear hyperbolic to us. Yet given the Stoic notion of the unity of the virtues, it follows that one who does not err in speech does not err in anything else. Philo indeed treated Moses as just such an individual, rare as he might be. For Philo Moses was the most perfect man because he was able perfectly to control his appetites and desires. Seneca imagines the same as possible (though of course rare)—a person who is 'undisturbed by fears, unspoiled by pleasures' and who know that 'death is no evil and that the gods are not powers of evil' (*Ep.* 75.17).

That James embraces the possibility of perfection is seen not only by 3:2, but by the opening *sorites* (Jas 1:2–4). A comparison of James with 1 Pet 1:6–7 and Rom 5:3–5 is instructive:

Rom 5:(1–2),3–5	1 Pet 1:6–7	Jas 1:2–4
1 ... we have peace with God through our Lord Jesus Christ,		
^{2} through whom we have obtained access to this grace in which we stand; and we boast in our hope of sharing the glory of God. ^{3} And not only that, but we also boast (*kauchaomai*) in our **sufferings** (*thlipeis*), knowing that **suffering** produces **endurance** (*hypomonē*), ^{4} and **endurance** produces **approval character** (*dokimē*), and **approval of character** produces **hope**, ^{5} and **hope** does not disappoint us, because God's love has been poured into our hearts through the Holy Spirit that has been given to us.	^{6} In this you shall rejoice (*agalliaomai*) if now for a little time, you must you suffer (*lypo*) variegated **trials** (*peirasmoi*), so that the **approval** (*to dokimon*) of your faith ... might be found to praiseworthy and reputable and honourable at the *apokalypsis* of Jesus Christ.	^{2} Consider it as pure joy (*chara*), my brothers, when you fall among variegated **trials** (*peirasmoi*), ^{3} knowing that the **approval** (*to dokimon*) of your faith produces **endurance** (*hypomonē*); ^{4} but let **endurance** have its full effect so that you might be **perfect** and whole, lacking in nothing.

The *sorites* in Romans is perfect, with a continuous chain of linked nouns—suffering–endurance–approval of character–hope. 1 Peter lacks a *sorites* entirely although as noted in Chapter 2, it displays a few other similarities to Jas 1:2–4. James *sorites* is defective—defective, because the link between trials and approval is only implied. Yet what is most striking is the final result of the chains: in Romans it is the hope of infusion by the spirit; in 1 Peter a praiseworthy character is the result; but in James it is perfection. In both Romans and 1 Peter, explicitly Christian ideas are prominent in the argumentative chain, either Christ's agency in conferring grace and the holy spirit, or the rewards of endurance that are to be expected at the *apokalypsis* of Christ. None of these Christological elements is present in James. The focus is only on the role of suffering in producing perfection.

The *Testament of Joseph* has a similar aetiology that involves testing, approval, and endurance:

> In ten testings (*peirasmoi*) [God] showed that I was approved (*dokimon*), and in all of these I was patient; for patience is a great medicine and endurance (*hypomonē*) produces many good things.
>
> (*T.Jos.* 2.7)

For both Philo and the Stoics endurance (*hypomonē*) is not passive, but rather active, and based on the knowledge that adversity and even death are not be feared (e.g., Philo, *Cherub.* 78; Seneca, *de constantia* 8.3). Musonius describes the endurance of testing as 'training':

> We use the training common to both [the body and the soul] when we discipline ourselves to cold, heat, thirst, hunger, meager rations, hard beds, avoidance of pleasures, and endurance under suffering. For by these things and others like them the body is strengthened and becomes capable of enduring hardship, sturdy and ready for any task; the soul too is strengthened, *since it is trained through endurance under hardship for courage, and for self-control by abstinence from pleasures.*
>
> (Musonius Rufus, *Diss.* 6)

For Philo, Seneca, Musonius, and for James (1:3), the ability to endure testing comes from knowledge that endurance plays a key role in the cultivation of a healthy soul.

The Emplanted Word

A final convergence with Stoicism (and Philo) has to do with James's reference to the implanted word (*emphytos logos*) in Jas 1:21. As is well known, Stoics held that Reason or Law was implanted in the cosmos such that it constitutes the law of nature which, if followed, leads to a happy life. Cicero, for example, says:

> Well then, the most learned men have determined to begin with Law, and it would seem that they are right, if, according to their definition, Law is the highest reason, implanted in Nature (*lex est ratio summa insita in natura*), which commands what ought to be done and forbids the opposite. This reason, when firmly fixed and fully developed in the human mind, is Law. And so they believe that Law is intelligence, whose natural function it is to command right conduct and forbid wrongdoing.
>
> (Cicero, *de Legibus* 1.18–19)

As Hindy Najman has shown, Philo equated this implanted law with the Law of Moses. The Mosaic laws are 'likenesses and copies of the patterns enshrined in the soul' (*Mos.* 2.11) and indeed rather paradoxically, written copies of the unwritten law (Najman 2010). Philo can account for Abraham's status as one who lived in full accordance with the Law, in spite of the fact that as Philo knew, Abraham lived before Moses and the giving of the Law. Abraham became 'a law [to himself] and an unwritten statute' (*Abr.* 276). With the giving of the Law, Moses, who was the perfect imitation of the law, became a model for all others.

Accepting that James's 'implanted word' converges with Stoic and Philonic notions of the natural law, Matt Jackson-McCabe has offered a reading that makes sense of Jas 1:21. The 'implanted word' reflects a philosophical notion of law, originally 'implanted' by God in humanity but especially available to James's addressees by virtue of their willingness to 'receive' or embrace the law and to live in accord with it (Jackson-McCabe 2001, 238). As Jas 1:12–22 makes clear, this is the opposite of being ruled by desire and anger. The implicit paradox, explained by Najman, is that all humanity has received the implanted *logos*; yet some—Jews and Christ followers—have been endowed in particular with the ability to live in accordance with it.

The convergences of James with Stoic psychology do not imply borrowing or 'influence'; they are convergences: points where James's perspective on testing, endurance, desire, and training and his notion of 'receiving' and implanted word make sense if seen in the broader context of Stoic psychology.

James and Paul

The issues raised in Jas 2:14–26 do not focus on the mastery of the self and the contrary tendencies that lurk within the self, but with the relation of deeds to faith. A question that has dogged exegetes since the time of Luther is whether James and Paul are at odds with one another, and whether Paul is reacting to James (which would require an early dating for James), or vice versa.

Jas 2:14–26 begins by assuming for argument's sake the distinction between faith (*pistis*) and deeds (*erga*). The thrust of James's argument, of course, is that the two cannot be separated. This distinction is peculiar and entirely foreign to second temple Judaism. *Pistis* in its ordinary sense is best rendered as 'faithfulness' or 'loyalty'. If rendered in this way, it is obvious that *pistis* cannot exist without an empirical demonstration of faithfulness or loyalty. 'Loyalty' without any evidence of loyalty is nothing (as James indeed argues).

James invokes the distinction only to rejects it. The only way to make sense of the argument in 2:14–26 is to see that James is invoking the distinction made *by Paul* in Galatians and Romans between *pistis* ('faith') and deeds (*erga*). Paul used these terms in a very particular way: the deed in question was the circumcision of males, and the faith in question was a faith in the redemptive power of Christ's death and resurrection. The distinction that James invokes only makes sense if we assume that he is referring to *Paul's* language of Galatians and Romans; no other Jew would make such a distinction.

There are other reasons for concluding that James is referring to Paul. Allison (2013b, 127) points out that Jas 2:14–26 shares with Paul expressions that rarely appear outside of Paul: 'to be justified from' (the aorist passive of *dikaioō* + *ek*: 6× in Paul); 'from faith' (*ek pisteōs*) (20× in Paul); and 'from deeds' (in the plural) (*ex ergōn*: 2× in Paul). That is, when these phrases appear in Jas 2:14–26, James is mimicking Paul's language.

Finally, as I have pointed out in Chapter 4, James, when referring to the Jewish Bible and the Jesus tradition, is more likely to paraphrase than to quote verbatim. This highlights the unusual nature of his verbatim citations. What is common to three of the four verbatim citations—Jas 2:8 (= Lev 19:18), Jas 2:11 (Deut 5:17–18), and Jas 2:23 (Gen 15:6)—is that they are all texts that Paul also cited verbatim. In Gal 5:14 and Rom 13:9 Paul cites Lev

19:18, arguing that the 'Golden rule' is a summary or epitome of the whole Law. Paul cites Deut 5:17–18 in the same context, asserting that the prohibitions of adultery, murder, theft, and covetousness ('and the other commandments') are subsumed and summarized by Lev 19:18. Paul cites Gen 15:6 in Gal 3:6 and Rom 4:3 to argue that Abraham was justified by faith and *not* from his deeds. As is very clear, James disagrees with each of these applications of texts from the Jewish Bible. He cites them verbatim to make the point that Paul's understanding is wrong: Lev 19:18 is not a summary of the Decalogue or of Leviticus 19 if that means ignoring other prescriptions; on the contrary, the righteous person is bound to observe each of the commandments. Both Abraham and Rahab were justified by what they did, and not simply what they believed. The example of Rahab for James proves the point, for Rahab is not said to have 'believed' at all. She acted to send the spies safely away. James resorts to verbatim citations when he is more disposed to paraphrase because *his point is exegetical*: Paul's understanding of these texts is wrong.

Given James's invocation of a Pauline distinction between faith and deeds, the appearances of Pauline phrases, and James's explicit citations of the OT texts that Paul also used, it is difficult to avoid the conclusion that James is writing with Paul in mind. The striking agreements between the two make it very unlikely that James and Paul were writing independently of one another. That does not mean that James is confronting Paul in the terms of Paul's arguments in Galatians and Romans, for Paul was expressly concerned with whether non-Jews could only be Christ followers by becoming Jews through proselyte practices. James shows no interest in these matters. Thus some scholars have argued that James was not confronting Paul at all, but only at distortions of Paul. Yet the fact that James explicitly cites Pauline formulations, and takes direct aim at the biblical quotations that Paul used in Galatians and Romans suggests rather strongly that James is confronting Paul directly (thus also Jackson-McCabe 2001, 243–53; Allison 2013b).

Conclusion

The peculiar features of the letter of James—its address to the Twelve Tribes in the diaspora—its lack of explicit reference of the distinctives of the Christ cult, its focus on the conditions of the soul, and its convergences with Stoicizing tendencies of Hellenistic Judaism, all receive a satisfactory explanation if we hypothesize that James was framed as the letter of a principal representative of the Jesus movement, but one reputed to be faithful to the Torah. The letter is almost certainly written in the diaspora and to an urban audience. It fictively addresses all diaspora Jews, but its actual readers were probably Jews in Alexandria or perhaps Rome. Philo of Alexandria shows that Stoicizing versions of piety had already found fertile ground in some parts of the diaspora.

A paraenetic letter, James is especially interested in the guidance of the soul, or psychagogy. The array of interests in psychagogy permits us to suggest a social location of James within those circles of educated or semi-educated Jews, undoubtedly urban, who understood the Torah to be consistent with the best of Greek philosophy, and indeed urged that the ideals of popularized Stoicism could best be met by adhering to the Torah, conceived as the 'law of perfect freedom' and the 'implanted *logos*'.

Further Reading and Literature Cited

On the addressees of James:

Allison, Dale C. 2013a. *A Critical and Exegetical Commentary on the Epistle of James*. ICC. New York and London: Bloomsbury.

Dibelius, Martin, and Heinrich Greeven. 1976. *James: A Commentary on the Epistle of James*. Translated by Michael A. Williams. Hermeneia. Philadelphia, PA: Fortress Press.

Deines, Rolland. 2014. 'God or Mammon? The Danger of Wealth in Jesus Tradition and in the Epistle of James'. Pages 25–66 in *Anthropologie und Ethik im Frühjudentum und im Neuen Testament*, edited by M. Konradt and E. Schläpfer. Tübingen: Mohr Siebeck.

Halévy, Joseph. 1914. 'Lettre d'un rabbin de Palestine égarée dans l'évangile'. *Revue sémitique d'épigraphie et d'histoire ancienne* 22: 197–201, 202–6.

Kloppenborg, John S. 1999. 'Patronage Avoidance in the Epistle of James'. *HvTS* 55.4: 755–94.

Massebieau, Louis. 1895. 'L'Épître de Jacques est-elle l'oeuvre d'un chrétien?' *RHR* 31–2: 249–83.

McNeile, Alan H. 1923. *New Testament Teaching in the Light of St. Paul's*. Cambridge: Cambridge University Press.

Sanfridson, Rebecca Runesson. 2018. 'Locating the Jacobean Community: A Comparative Study of Economic Survival and Conflict Management in the Letter of James and Ancient Mediterranean Associations'. Thesis (M.Th.). St. Andrew's University.

On the 'Twelve Tribes of the Diaspora'

Mayor, Joseph B. 1892. *The Epistle of St. James: The Greek Text with Introduction, Notes and Comments.* London: Macmillan.
Sanders, E. P. 1992. *Judaism: Practice and Belief 63 BCE–66 CE.* Philadelphia, PA: Trinity Press International.

Literature with 'double addressees'

Allison, Dale C. 2001.'The Fiction of James and Its *Sitz im Leben*'. *RB* 108.4: 529–70. DOI: 10.44089570.
Kloppenborg, John S. 2007. 'Judaeans or Judean Christians in James'. Pages 113–35 in *Identity and Interaction in the Ancient Mediterranean: Jews, Christians and Others.* Edited by P. Harland and Z. A. Crook. New Testament Monographs 18. London and New York: Sheffield-Phoenix.
Lincoln, Bruce. 2006. *Holy Terrors: Thinking about Religion after September 11.* Chicago, IL: University of Chicago Press.

On 4QMMT and its possible relevant to James

García Martínez, Florentino, and Eibert J. C. Tigchelaar. 1997. *The Dead Sea Scrolls Study Edition.* Leiden: Brill.
Collins, John J. 1997. 'Expectation of the End in the Dead Sea Scrolls'. Pages 74–90 in *Eschatology, Messianism, and the Dead Sea Scrolls.* Edited by C. A. Evans and P. W. Flint. Studies in the Dead Sea Scrolls and Related Literature. Grand Rapids, MI: Eerdmans.

The Urban Jesus Movement, Rich and Poor

Batten, Alicia J. 2014. 'The Urbanization of Jesus Traditions in James'. Pages 78–96 in *James, 1 & 2 Peter and the Early Jesus Tradition.* Edited by A. Batten and J. S. Kloppenborg. LNTS 478. London and New York: Bloomsbury T&T Clark.
Kloppenborg, John S. 2019. *Christ's Associations: Connecting and Belonging in the Ancient City.* New Haven, CT: Yale University Press.
Maynard-Reid, Pedrito U. 1987. *Poverty and Wealth in James.* Maryknoll, NY: Orbis Books.

Meeks, Wayne A. 1983. *The First Urban Christians: The Social World of the Apostle Paul*. New Haven, CT: Yale University Press.

Philosophical Influences on Hellenistic Judaism and James

Jackson-McCabe, Matt A. 2001. *Logos and Law in the Letter of James: The Law of Nature, the Law of Moses, and the Law of Freedom.* NovTSup 100. Leiden: Brill.

Kloppenborg, John S. 2010. 'James 1:2–15 and Hellenistic Psychagogy'. *NovT* 52.1: 37–71. DOI: 10.1163/004810010X12577565604134.

Najman, Hindy. 2010. 'A Written Copy of the Law of Nature: An Unthinkable Paradox?' Pages 107–18 in *Past Renewals: Interpretative Authority, Renewed Revelation and the Quest for Perfection in Jewish Antiquity*. Supplements to the Journal for the Study of Judaism 53. Leiden: Brill.

Reydams-Schils, Gretchen J. 2005. *The Roman Stoics: Self, Responsibility, and Affection*. Chicago, IL: University of Chicago Press.
An excellent introduction to the kind of Stoicism current in the early Principate, and which may have influenced Philo.

On James 2:14–26: The literature is vast and every commentary on James devotes considerable space to this pericope.

Allison, Dale C. 2013b. 'Jas 2: 14–26: Polemic against Paul, Apology for James'. Pages 123–49 in *Ancient Perspectives on Paul*. Edited by T. Nicklas, A. Merkt, and J. Verheyden. Novum Testamentum et Orbis Antiquus / Studien zur Umwelt des Neuen Testaments 102. Göttingen: Vandenhoeck & Ruprecht.

Kloppenborg, John S. 2020. 'Verbatim Citations in James'. Pages 254–69 in *'To Recover What Has Been Lost': Essays on Eschatology, Intertextuality, and Reception History in Honor of Dale C. Allison Jr.* Edited by T. Ferda, D. Frayer-Griggs, and N. Johnson. NovTSup 183. Leiden: Brill. DOI: 10.1163/9789004444010_015.

EPILOGUE: THE
LEGACY OF JAMES

As I have explained in Chapter 2, the evidence for the existence of James prior to the first quarter of the third century CE is nonexistent. This is what leads to the suspicions that were cast on the authenticity of the letter. No one prior to the sixteenth century appears to have seen any potential conflicts with Paul's views. The suspicions about James seem to have arisen solely because it was simply unknown in the first century and for most of the second.

By the time James entered circulation in the third century and been accepted as authoritative, there was little likelihood that it would be viewed as a counterpoint to Paul. The widespread conviction that scripture could not in principle be self-contradictory was simply too strong. Origen's commentary on Romans cited James a dozen times without ever hinting at any tension between James and Paul.

One might have suspected that in the early fifth century Pelagius and Augustine would have squared off over James. But this did not occur. In his *Expositio ad Romanos* (3.28) Pelagius commented on Rom 3:28 ('a person is justified by faith apart from works of the Law') and 1 Cor 13:2, which privileged love over faith. Pelagius saw a possible conflict, but it could be resolved easily, Pelagius argued, by understanding the 'works of the law' as circumcision and Sabbath laws. When 'the blessed James' asserted that 'faith without works is dead' (Jas 2:26), he was speaking of the 'works of justice' not the 'works of the Laws'.

For this part, Augustine cited James in support of Paul's views. In Augustine's view, although faith as a gift of God could not earned through good deeds, the faith that did not produce good deeds was worthless. On the contrary, genuine faith

is the faith which separates the faithful of God from the unclean demons. For they too, as the apostle James says, 'believe and tremble' [Jas 2:19], but they do not do good deeds. They, therefore, do not have the faith from which the righteous live, that is, the faith which works through love, so that God gives them eternal life in accord with their works.

(De gratia et libero arbitrio 7.17–18; Yates 2002, 287)

For most of the time between Augustine and the sixteenth century, James and Paul were seen as being in essential agreement. In view of this strong tendency to harmonize James with Paul, it is striking how different was the approach to James in the sixteenth century. Erasmus and Cajetans revived earlier doubts about the authorship of James (see above, Chapter 2) but this did not lead them to reject the canonicity of James. It is only with Luther that James's apostolic authority came into question, especially after 1519. Luther's 1515 *Lectures on Romans* initially took a view of the relationship between Paul and James not unlike that of Origen: Paul distinguished between the efficacy of faith *versus* the works of the Law, but James was speaking of the works of faith, that is, the deeds that follow from genuine faith (*Lectures on Romans*, on Rom 3:20; WA 56).

This changed dramatically after the 1519 the debate with Johannes Eck at which, pressed by Eck's quotation of Jas 2:17, Luther replied with a version of Erasmus's critique of James: it did not evince the dignity of an apostle. By 1522, in the *Preface to the New Testament*, Luther had claimed James as an 'epistle of straw' and the same year he had articulated substantial arguments against Jacobean authorship (*Preface to the Epistles of James and Jude*). His most immoderate claims, that James was authored by 'some Jew' (1542), and that it should be thrown into the oven (1546), came only in the last years of Luther's life (d. 1546).

Luther's views of James had long-lasting impact. Zwingli defended Jacobean authorship and reconciled James with Paul much in the same way that Augustine had proposed. Calvin doubted Jacobean authorship but nonetheless upheld the authority of the letter and saw no contradiction between Paul's and James's respective views of faith (George 2000). Luther's negative views of James persisted in many circles, however, so much so that several editions of the New Testament followed Luther's lead in placing Hebrews, James, Jude, and Revelation as a kind of codicil, at the end of the New Testament instead of placing James along with the other Catholic letters.

Negative evaluations of James's Christian identity continued well into the twentieth century. Jülicher pronounced it to be the 'least Christian book in the New Testament' (Jülicher 1904, 225) and for Bultmann, perhaps the most influential exegete-theologian of the twentieth century, James lacked 'every shred of understanding for the Christian's situation'. He even toyed with the idea that James was a lightly edited Jewish document (Bultmann 1951–1955, 2:162–163).

James, however, has other legacies. James was a favourite text of Søren Kierkegaard, often understood to be the father of existential philosophy. Kierkegaard complained of the tendency of the Lutheranism of his day to turn the gospel and grace into a set of laws even more rigorous than the old law (Kierkegaard assumed the classical Lutheran distinction between 'law' [Old Testament] and 'gospel' [New Testament]). This could have led him to revise Pauline theology. But Kierkegaard also disliked the tendency of those who studied the Bible to focus on doctrines rather and seeing study as a personal encounter. It was James's metaphor of mirror (Jas 1:23) that epitomized for Kierkegaard the true relationship between the individual and the Bible:

> If God's Word is for you merely a doctrine, something impersonal and objective, then it is no mirror—an objective doctrine cannot be called a mirror; it is just as impossible to look at yourself in an objective doctrine as to look at yourself in a wall. And if you want to relate impersonally (objectively) to God's Word, there can be no question of looking at yourself in the mirror, because it takes a personality, an 'I', to look at oneself in a mirror; a wall can be seen in a mirror, but a wall cannot see itself or look at itself in a mirror. No, while reading God's Word you must incessantly say to yourself: It is I to whom it is speaking; it is I about whom it is speaking.
>
> (Kierkegaard 1851/1990, 43–4)

At almost the same time as Kierkegaard, Frederick Douglass in the United States drew on James for a very different purpose. Douglass, a former slave and eloquent advocate of abolitionism frequently quoted James in his sermons. Jas 1:27 provided for him the best summary of pure and undefiled piety: 'to care for orphans and widows in their distress, to keep oneself unblemished by the world'. Jas 3:17 was also one of his favourite texts: 'the wisdom that comes from above is first, pure, then peaceful, obedient, full of mercy and good fruit, impartial, not hypocritical'. His point was to underscore the incommensurability of slave-owning Christianity with James's view of pure and undefiled piety. A piety that favours the rich over the poor and the proud over the humble cannot be claimed as 'pure and undefiled religion' (see Amyer 2008).

With the advent of liberation theology in the 1970s and 1980s, James's critique of wealth also attracted much attention. James came to serve as one of the main supports for the 'preferential option for the poor', the insistence that Christian teaching and practice must be oriented to the needs of the poor and marginalized. It was critical, Elsa Tamez (2002) urged, that James's discourse on rich and poor not be domesticated and rendered comfortable by understanding the poor as 'spiritually poor', as might happen if one relied solely on Matthew's Sermon on the Mount. In James, the 'poor' were those without resources, and the rich were those who abused the poor. Taking James seriously meant confronting real economic disparities and injustices. When James is read by persons in the Third World, it became a pungent criticism of wealth and privilege and of the wealthy and their privilege.

Novelist Upton Sinclair (*The Profits of Religion*) reports that he once read Jas 5:1–5 to a group of ministers, and attributed those words to Emma Goldman, the famous anarchist and political critic. Without recognizing the actual source of the quotation, these ministers immediately called for Goldman's deportation. James continues to win friends and to irritate.

Further Reading and Literature Cited

On the history of the interpretation of James:

Aymer, Margaret P. 2008. *First Pure, Then Peaceable: Frederick Douglass Reads James*. LNTS 379. London and New York: T&T Clark.

Bauckham, Richard J. 1999. *James: Wisdom of James, Disciple of Jesus the Sage*. New Testament Readings. London and New York: Routledge.
This is perhaps the best treatment of James and his legacy in Kierkegaard. Bauckham prefaces each chapter with an epigram from Kierkegaard and devotes the final chapter to 'Reading James in nineteenth-century Copenhagen'.

Bultmann, Rudolf K. 1951–1955. *Theology of the New Testament.*
    Translated by K. Grobel. New York: Scribners.
Felder, Cain Hope. 1982–83. 'Partiality and God's Law: An Exegesis of
    James 2: 1–13'. *JRT* 39: 51–69.
George, Timothy. 2000. '"A Right Strawy Epistle." Reformation
    Perspectives on James'. *Southern Baptist Journal of Theology* 4: 20–31.
    A remarkably clear account of James in the development of Luther's
    thought, and the reactions to Luther among Zwingli, Calvin, and the
    Anabaptists.
Gowler, David B. 2013. *James through the Centuries.* Oxford and Walden:
    Wiley Blackwell.
    Gowler illustrates the history of the interpretation of James not only
    through literary sources but with icons, mediaeval woodcuts, hymns,
    and political polemics.
Jülicher, Adolf. 1904. *An Introduction to the New Testament.* Translated
    by J. Penrose Ward. London: Smith, Elder.
Kierkegaard, Søren. 1990 [1851]. 'James, Chapter I, v. 22 to the End
    [1851]'. Pages 7–51 in *Kierkegaard's Writings, XXI: For Self-
    Examination / Judge for Yourself!* Edited by Howard V. Hong and
    Edna H. Hong. Princeton, NJ: Princeton University Press.
Tamez, Elsa. 2002. *The Scandalous Message of James: Faith without
    Works Is Dead.* Revised edition. New York: Crossroad.
Yates, Jonathan P. 2002. 'The Epistle of James in Augustine and His
    Pelagian Adversaries: Some Preliminary Observations'. *Augustiniana*
    52.2/4: 273–90.

INDEX OF REFERENCES

Page numbers in bold type indicate a significant discussion of that text

5122 INDEX OF REFERENCES

INDEX OF SPECIAL VOCABULARY

INDEX OF MODERN AUTHORS